ALSO BY NATHANIEL TARN

Old Savage/Young City, 1964
Selection: Penguin Modern Poets No. 7, 1965
Where Babylon Ends, 1968
The Beautiful Contradictions, 1969
October, 1969
The Silence, 1969
A Nowhere for Vallejo, 1971
Section: The Artemision, 1973
The Persephones, 1974
Lyrics for the Bride of God, 1975
Narrative of this Fall, 1975

TRANSLATIONS

The Heights of Macchu Picchu (Pablo Neruda), 1966
Con Cuba, 1969
Stelae (Victor Segalen), 1969
Selected Poems (Pablo Neruda), 1970

NATHANIEL TARN

THE

HOUSE

OF

LEAVES

Santa Barbara
Black Sparrow Press
1976

ACKNOWLEDGEMENT

Some of the poems in this book first appeared in *Ambit, Anonym, Beliot Poetry Journal, Books Abroad, Boundary Two, Credences, Desert Rune, Famous, The Scotsman, Stooge, The, Via,* and *Toothpick, Lisbon, & the Orcas Islands,* to whose editors grateful acknowledgment is made.

LIBRARY OF CONGRESS CATALOGING IN PUBLICATION DATA

Tarn, Nathaniel.
    The house of leaves.

    I. Title.
PR6070.A57H6   1976   821'.9'14   76-19090
ISBN 0-87685-260-6
ISBN 0-87685-259-2 pbk.

"To Everybody"

Andrea Tarn, 1776

TABLE OF CONTENTS

ONE
ONE
ONE
ONE
ONE
ONE
ONE
ONE
ONE
ONE
ONE
ONE
ONE
ONE
ONE
ONE
ONE
ONE
ONE
ONE
ONE
ONEONE
ONE
ONE
ONE
ONE
ONE
ONE
ONE
ONE
ONE
ONE

LETTER FROM LENINGRAD TO THE REASON FOR LIVING

for Arnold and Dusty Wesker

Words like worms in a corpse
I cannot see them   yet feel them near
they move at the tip of my fingers
their taste   hovers   on my tongue
they curl round my eyes   inside my ears
                demanding audience

Conversation done   blur of bus windows
halfway from Novgorod   stop in the fields
piss in a haze of huge mosquitoes
and the flat earth of Russia stretches out
from the Baltic to the Japan Sea
                green here, underfoot

There is so much to understand
the fattest catkins you can imagine
Prague   Bratislava   the Initial Peace
but here the speeches   gold on red medallions
1917 in cyphers   bleeding glass
                and movement petrified

   I dream that I have died
   I am told to walk into heaven
   which is a palace of glass
   I am to talk to no one
   but to walk straight ahead
   many others are doing the same
   . . . after many hours
   many days of walking
   asking what it's all about
   (my father dead before me
   younger than I at that

unable to answer)
I come to a wall
on the other side of which
there is another heaven
but only a very few
highly placed persons go over
look around   come back again

The resurrection crystallizes around Him
white on His white star
the curve is made straight
the circle squared
the disciples thrown on frozen spittle
                    in molten sleep

A cloud of brimstone   curling
assaults the sleeping Virgin
Dove rocking on a stream of blood
out of the weeping brimstone
above the angel whose wings
                    span all of Russia

The fattest catkins you can imagine
tongued into patterns   her lower hair
on shining thigh   medusa's dial
the snake mouth opens
I enter in   her namelessness
                    music heard about here

I began as a pastoral poem
    there was a hawk on a telephone pole
        warblers in willows calling me where I could not go
            new whips of growth on the pines, another green
                buttercups like the galaxies of each other
                    a small brown flower with an earthquake heart
                        an eternity of birches

I lie in a field on the edges of
    the long white nights of Leningrad

12

in the arms of a dream I have of her
        and perhaps it is because of all those golden domes
            the grass makes patterns on our drowning backs
                willow seed raining sperm in the still, still air
                        from the fattest catkins you could ever imagine

The hungry land stretches out its arms
crying with all its rivers
and I cannot ever let go of her long body
imagine: and there is no more time
Penjamo sixty-two
                will solve it all

Anatole talking thru the night
burning manuscripts
blue-bound   smell of sardines
a gifted icon rocking in my arms
Sasha showing his ring: Gräf   Gräf
                we are both Barons

They fetch me in the cavernous hotel
addresses go flushing down the toilet
Boris   minus two legs
fucks a fat blonde behind a wall of sheets
Sasha uses her mouth
                his ring still glinting

Her cunt gleams in the dark
behind the golden balls of Boris
we leap on elegant horses
in pale 17th century colors
to kick out the sockets
                of the mother of Russia

There is so much to understand
        and I want   as always   to talk to you about it
            stored up for you until the load of days crushes
                imagine: and there is no more time
                        the ice cap spreads   the world is starving

there is ice on the silk of her thighs
the man-made stars slip slowly from our visio

Two weeks from now Prague will fall silent

this tide shall turn . . .

FOOD

for Lucien Biton

From a thousand years back
    he talks of the grass
which must be covered with salt
    from sea-spray
to make good lamb,
             the elements
of food-philosophy—

      talks of the time before
which is always better of course,
      the art of life
passage of life thru life
      and its digestion
coming together,   blending of substances
      in their proper order

      taste of the world
being nothing else than taste of world
        you have under your nose
    odor of blood
    rare / medium / well
    odor of green beans
    odor of goat
the lining of the stomach
      jewelled with wine:
civilization

    and a geography:
      of the city
        of the appropriate places
in which to purchase the ingredients:
      (black-legged pullet of Nantes

blue-skinned, difficult to pluck,
small one of Bresse, made
to be worked on, to be simmered
in cream—well into Normandy
par exemple)

a demography:
But no cooking in OUR country
no working of the food / only for paupers
the complications of soup: & nothing, ever, boiled
except for once a year to please the kids
& the tail-end of peasant in our souls you see . . .

a memorial:
in my country, when kids left the house,
O Loire de Ronsard et la chair attendrie,
the individual soup-dish left as well
& here is my dish & here is my wife's
—charming little objects, complex, covered,—
how shall they come again ever

the good times
before she died?

Brief burst of tears
into the wine, the dilution,
memory of a hard time
the breast gone, the dug, and still needed
even at seventy
(I cry daily he says everyday)

IN THE CAPITAL, he begins again,
everything is dying,
you can't find the right ingredients
any more
yes, well, I'm sure of *my* cheeses
but the strawberries are made by engineers,
I'm sure of the string beans
but the cutlets are doubtful

(elsewhere than in *my* shop
  the very CUT
  the structure of the piece of meat
  O Lévi-Strauss!
  gone out of memory of living men . . .)
Then the flood
     the encyclopaedic memorandum
           the perfection of wisdom
the brain,   three times the speed of anyone I know

in the skull
    oiled by wine and cognac
         self-owned beyond all else:

      THE INTELLECT!

    and now go tell
    those who take food
    and freeze it to death
    before it ever
    reaches the right store
      the right street in the city
        the correct degree of the oven
            the erotic mind . . .

THREE PORTRAITS

1: RENE MAGRITTE

for John Digby

A long time coming   fame

        question of levels
        under the sea a forest
        under the forest rooms   rooms   floors

the heart of mathematics
repeat   repeat
call one   now vary

        we are responsible for this whole universe
        but decide nothing in it
        (save only love)

this   love
this love
time   walking with her legs into the picture

        her back within her belly
        careful to show
        the prowling hair

window   coming in at the seams
but did not try the buttock/breast analogy
yet must have guessed it

apple   ball   two balls
the semiotic liquid
in that round belly only   like the Dutch painters

fish
fuckable fish
with the backdrop Tristan's

     the suck of fire
     the brass of it
     butterflies breathing

and the eagles of Arnhem
and the egg
laid by the mountains

2: ANTON BRUCKNER

for Jack Collom

Laid in his sheets
thin ship   locked in pack snow
with dirty margins
an animal   broken into a field
and yet no blood
            to flow
                   to charm the barrens

to poppy
        wheat
            and grass
as in that music
   that organ growl
       an architecture
              spire-born

    All that is linear
with the intolerable patience of music
the long dwelling on time   the inaudible variation
the ear   straining to break the music   and the music not
breaking one moment from the furrow
    he thought he heard an angel smile
              noiseless   within the music

The city full of laughter
           criticism
           witticism

at his expense
the city laying down the law
          from all its spires

from all its clocks
and he   wanting to know
the disposition   the fingering of time

the matter of the clock   the angels round it
who counted prayers   sweet simpleton
                    in missal margins

glimpsed girls
            frightened at glimpsing him
feared out of true

Alone
      with pension
with certificates
      proven good conduct
the way to God
            letting time work

            letting the long line work its voices all the time
            no one could tell it from monotony
            because he looked backwards
            and found eternity there
                  the quick
                        quick mouse
                  and had no time for futures

dear humility
dear   dear humility
dear repetition

but the world is like that   do you not see it
do you not hear it   but the world is like that
            different   same

In a time of wrath
in the time of Anti-Christ
wrath spreading like a shroud
                  with dirty margins

they speak the words
in the same voices
their laughter echoes in the domes

       certificates

but that is not the sound I hear

            out there   I own the music

3: ANTONIN ARTAUD

for Elton and Gail Anglada

In this complexion
I know I need not know what follows here
the problem solved forever
                              but you turned away

I do request the pleasure of your company

and could have had   many a happy year
I have no doubt   made a career
at last in some approximation to myself
                              but this is not

what he designed me for

We either act in hope
or hope the world will act
all by itself and all at once
                              to break old uncle negativity

his lousy spine

Ahme   Ahme   Ah Mexico
will yield this secret
I know that we shall lose
                    omens / omens

but you turned away

              Give you   the unity of all this life

In fields   in deserts
gardens reduced to deserts   where the sand glows

where the sun mimes acres of wheat
                        green fingers reach above the wheat

this idyll

our ageing bodies detach the light
and draw it to themselves like covering
leaving transparent
                        the wound of wrinkles

and her mouth to my door in my own house

She had placed her hand on my head
and in my privileged state
I had thought   Hebrides
                        Skye the other said   sky
Acoma   Acoma   sky city

No place that I have ever reached
out distances this love
I have called back
                        all chartered borders

maintaining inequality
while I proclaim the love of all mankind
what else is there to do but on and on
                        work without residue

without forgiveness
        and say no
to body only body
                        to spirit only spirit

I plunged in you $\dfrac{up}{down}$ to my elbows

                        but you turned away

AFTER JOUVE

for Henri and No Seigle

Think a little of the sun in your youth
The sun which shone when you were ten years old
Surprise do you remember the sun in your youth
If you focus your eyes well
Watch narrowly
You can still catch a glimpse of it
It was pink
It took up half the sky
You could look at it straight in the face you could
Surprise but it was so straightforward
It had a color
A dance it had desire
A heat
An extraordinary ease
It loved you
All that in the middle of your age sometimes
   running on rails along the morning's forests
You thought you imagined
Deep in yourself
It's in the heart that the old suns are put away
It has not moved there is that sun
Of course yes there it is
I have lived I have ruled
I illuminated with such a great sun
Alas it's dead
Alas it has never
Been
Oh that sun you say
And yet your youth was unhappy

. . . .

There's no need to be king of Jerusalem

Every life questions itself
       Every life asks itself
                And every life waits
Every man travels the same way everything is limited
    how to see more
And we went and invented ourselves machines
They came smashing everything drilling the old earth
    filling the old air
Waves rays shining axes
And there you are my power has grown terrible
My anxiety also
My instability
I can't sit still any more
I search I become
I'm no longer my real age I toy with everything
But my God hoary war has come back and scarcely changed
Human blood has only one way of flowing
Death has only one way of flowing
Death has only one step always the same to fall upon me
Has its mask changed must be the wax
Space has shrunk my soul is it newer
I do not say better
I would not dare

. . . .

We are far from stewing in resignation but
Our pleasure is always the guiltiest
For if grief should need justification grief is the earth
    our city grows on
Joy purity
Don't come near
It's in relation to our joy
That our vanity seems so pitiful
We're in such a rush
Our doubts are so old
Yes it's with our joy that we tremble
Degenerate child
Yet the spirit suspended over universal sorrow
Said you have senses make them give back your pleasure

And that is bitter
More bitter
And that speeds up somehow in bitterness
For us

. . . .

Eternal Judge
What power stupidity has the stars shine for stupidity
Light suits it so well the great trains take it everywhere
Every town is its meeting place its pleasure park
And on sundays one catches sight of its family picnic
What glory after the war
For disorder and lightheartedness
Everyone lives so much better
What an achievement for the boxer
The poet
Still lives on the fifth floor ailing of an old hunger
Meditates on his approaching death looking to be eternal
No don't think he loves death as he used to love it
He asks questions
He tries groping
He sighs he is delirious
And life he thinks would be really marvelous if

. . . .

The greatest business is dying and we don't know
    a jot of it
Those who came by don't come again
But I must admit that I'm not anxious
I no longer believe in them now
Without understanding I wipe them out they are dead
Oh silence
Complicity
Perhaps it isn't a business after all perhaps death
    is nothing to us
Or yet again perhaps

Everything is for this only death this great gateway
    this favored haven
Where the ship comes home
But no for I don't believe in happiness and I don't believe
    in death
I must tell you that I am ultimately certain of being immortal
Essential vanity

. . . .

When young I loved time
I couldn't stand being the youngest
I loved the grass when it seeded the trees
    when they spread themselves like music
I loved the old
Now I shadow the other side of the hill
The downward slope
I no longer know I've tasted many eras
Calm will come perhaps with age

. . . .

How much contempt man has for this mouth he adores
But he's found extasy there he goes on running after extasy
Vitality
He goes on demanding the smell taste and color
    of womens' bodies
Their elasticity
Their lie
Whatever in their mother-of-pearl flesh smiles chastely
    at death
And then after that
His sadness comes
Which he recognizes

. . . .

How hard we've searched—miracles we are miracles
Nothing
This world was straight infinite now it is curved
    slipping one into the other
Man's vision has grown but it is backed by less and less

Thought is thin feeble useless a trail of mist like the Milky Way
    like the Milky Way
While the world is matter is spread out is terrifying
    is real like the wall of hell
Thought smiles because it is going to die it could be

. . . .

These opposing stars
One which lit the fire and one which was lit by the fire
He who gave and she who asked action and mystery
He who throws and she who gestates are always present
    at whatever moment
Herald and Hunted swirl in the blue egg of space he and she
Then reunited
They make up a long song with heights and depths
Always falls always springs
They go back as they had come
Always the wave-shaped curve the heights and depths
There that's all
And the sea's hem the leaves' thrust the terrestrial fanfare
    of mountains
Don't be afraid of your sadness it is mine
It is ours it his his it is hers
Oh grandeur
Be not afraid here is peace life life is admirable
Life is vain
Life is admirable life is admirable it is vain

TWO
TWO
TWO
TWO
TWO
TWO
TWO
TWO
TWO
TWO
TWO
TWO
TWO
TWO
TWO
TWO
TWO
TWO
TWO
TWO
TWO
TWO
TWO
TWO
TWO
TWO
TWOTWO
TWO
TWO
TWO
TWO
TWO
TWO
TWO
TWO
TWO
TWO

THE ROSES OF GUATEMALA

for George and Lo Holton

La sanjuanera   yellow / brown / purple / red
   knees in a mould   striped
   bundle of grace
         continent whose essence is earth
            drawing men by the feet
       keeping them down
           by soles and heels

  among her roses like their lungs
       their hearts
     the silences they speak

roses transmuted into blood
    the china teas
    roses of a pink
        so astonishing
       they light a room with their own light

    compact
       placental
          fresh from the mist
      in the corn's nostrils
            barrancas
   deep-bellied rivers
       clouds
          deer and houndings

related to
    passions of understanding
           struck in
             earth's ore

At the market's heart
             fountain of loam
             aimed at the sky
       quadrilateral
       the best produce of Guatemala
                    from every star

to be consumed by?
    but   the whites of course
             los ladinos   who else?
    that tragedy
             insulated from the people
             by thin layers of hate
                    the lexicon thereof

    I talk to Pablo / Juan / Martin
                    met in a bus
    on the way to the capital
       They watch that peaceable kingdom
             one in uniform / one in plain clothes
                    car at the corner
    until I split.

THE CHURCH, SANTIAGO

for Andrée Brugcsh

The walls are standing
               you can see
thru windows in the walls
                  buttresses
still flying
          stone muscles

and the tower
        with its banner
and the motto on the banner
           about walls not falling
about walls hemming in
          what's inside

in a tongue I don't know anymore
            nor anyone
about
        having asked them once
   long ago
             forgotten

altar flat
    pulpit flat
        font flat
           chairs flat
       candles flat
    flowers flat

no priests
  no worshippers
          charity undone
   saint-cases empty

wood stacked in corners
        owners at home

no mail from God
        no messages from angels
                no annunciation
Gabriel tired
        Virgin wilting
           Holy Ghost awash

Ask them
  if you see them
      what stands in wind
blowing great conches
        alone in the center
      refusing to fall

has never told
     its mortal secret
        to any living thing
    or dead they say
        out there among crosses
in midnight rain.

RECEIPTS

for Kenneth Rexroth

Dark nights by the shore
    they were throwing the papers into the water
names were fading   dissolving in the water
         writing to ink   ink to water
    her eyes remembering the names

    Taken into the hills
had admired poinsettias in passing
       before the eyes were bandaged
  brushed and grazed by stones
         the thwarted light a darker grey sometimes
as they passed thru tunnels
           and birds remembered in the trees
          rats in their holes
      snakes among rocks
        she at the water
             but men   not

Small employments   not paying much
         jobs scarcely recorded
            else than statistically
    such men fired by the dozen
figures   names   security numbers   water to water
       whenever trees rained white blossom
    or some years pink

    now the captains
those who stood out   could be identified
         why   sometimes   in the uniforms of order
    you could hardly tell why they had agreed sometimes
       signed the soup-stained papers
   marched thru the hills

       sunk their securities

but those who had it worst were the *jefes*
     the few who might default
   stars in the public eye at every moment
      rewards conspicuous
the marches they went on
       so highly classified
no one ever knew
     at the end of the march a cavern
in which the other leaders judged them in secret
    when they went back into the world
  their papers were not even drowned
    did not go back into the water

and she who had watched the water
    her hands were light too soon

   they became unemployable little by little
     no one   including themselves
  knew exactly they had fallen from grace
     honor seemed expensive
they would be called on abruptly to prove it in themselves
  sometimes it hardly seemed worth the energy
    the incalculable price
     except   perhaps
     the pets were kinder

the change seemed very difficult to carry thru

DESDE PACHICHIYUT

for Gary Snyder

1.

Bait the trap for my voice   hear
    sad animals baying at the moon

If I could catch that beast
    come to the trap at leisure
study shape   fur
         color of eyes
blood   density of blood
    all its metabolisms

Not a hair in the trap
    whisker
urine   defecation
no faintest smell of passage

The animal
    if animal there is
is never seen alive
    never seen to die
    I shall not meet it I think
this side my life

Yet its ghost in me
      snarls suddenly & bites

    The trap is broken

2.

Over my shoulder
men and women passing

to market ∕ from market
on the mountain's side
commerce the whole of life

In front of me
flowers   books
an incense burner
beyond the terrace
plants   geranium fires
the cloth of waters far as I can see
silent canoes
lying about their size
the two breasts of the land

I have nothing to do
but to look at my life
two eyes   a microscope
but time eludes me

Power drains out
the poems melt
and as I look
at the sustained efforts of others
my weaknesses appear
like evening spiders

3.

Wake up in the night
     miss her bitterly
my hands on the various bodies
     quiver of senses

morning star struggles faintly
     with first weak light
light of oyster linings
     her cold blue lips

warming to answer

I hear her voice
    in the foreign accents
of the workers at my back
    going to maize

giving herself away
    in all her different guises
loading heavy requirements
    on the day's back

sitting in every canoe
passing my house far off
    without stopping

4.

Orchids lungeing like stars
    or springing spiders

six cents worth of carnations
six bunches   pink / red / white
    housing a single yellow rose

in the corner   bamboo   asleep
    spears no one uses

bunch of fleshly flowers
    whose name I can't find out
all the colors of fire

gardens   within and without
    speak to each other
under a single pink cloud

    hermit's delight

5.

The bird with a yellow breast
        thought to be melodious
does indeed / at last / gargle in sight

I have a book of birds
        pertaining to another country
—there are some migrations—

Thus: Eastern Bluebird
        I know his sapphire flight
when he marries the morning

Thus: Common Ground Dove
        I know her chestnut wings
and her wind moan

The little critters   in the aviary
of the conifers below the terrace
        may be Magnolia Warblers

Half-blind   I know the Humming Bird
woken by his bumblebee buzzing
        ballet among the flowers

Minimal Ornithology   Blessed Ignorance

6.

Long line of cloud along volcanos
        cuts dusk in half
shroud of rain over cone
        Volcan San Pedro

So still you can hear voices
        on boats half across the lake
lights on the other shore
        violent stars

Her name is Absence
        by definition

Here all is flame
the tropicals I can't identify
three candles burning in each room
my mind in its own stillness

Last night   was cut in half
        by vicious dreams
this ignorance of her true fate
        little news of her times

When will life mend?   When can I sew
        the halves together?

7.

Rats   all night long
        rustle of papers
in the morning   shit
                pungency

Lock myself into house
        lock keys in suitcase
cannot emerge
        at any level

Diary lost
camera stolen
recorder stolen
binoculars stolen
new camera dropped
conspiracy against
my recording time

Sun-stone for grinding maize
        purchased at last

tho ill-afforded
    sits in the hand
ovoid
    ridges for fingers

Grind problems suddenly
    with quiet joy
patience
    the life will out

Cards will come clean

8.

Learning
    by reference to others
copying out
    whole sentences
        taking my time
instead of rushing thru
  a book to say   I've read it
  and tho it's true I've read it
    bottom's dropped out
forgotten ╱
    no residue

Now
      painfully
  a library of books
built brick by brick
  not grave by grave

9.

Coming home
    things bought at market
to a bare house
    inhabitable now
with their simplicity

with night falling
on hushed dogs
        and grumbling dogs
rain   crying out its heart
        or the land's heart
rain spattering
        on warm roofs
the gladness of a desk
        about to be worn in
and the books waiting

        full of good lives

10.

Quietly
    life shatters
    pieces shared out
apportion this to X
        and that to Y
find little for myself

I do not think
God's in this world
Nobody's seen him
in this family
I don't think
he exists
My daughter
London   1966

As if I had gone off
        in the night
while the sharing was being performed
        and had forgotten

        to make a note of it

THREE
THREE
THREE
THREE
THREE
THREE
THREE
THREE
THREE
THREE
THREE
THREE
THREE
THREE
THREE
THREE
THREE
THREE
THREE
THREE
THREE
THREE
THREE
THREE
THREE
THREE
THREETHREE
THREE
THREE
THREE
THREE
THREE
THREE
THREE
THREE
THREE
THREE

WIND RIVER BALLAD

Wind River O Wind River
tonight I go to my Bride
Wind River O Wind River
tonight she lies by my side
and all your mountains and all your lakes
and all your bushes and trees
will sound like silence to the noise she makes
with her innumerable bees

Wind River O Wind River
tonight I taste of her breast
Wind River O Wind River
her milk is the milk of the blest
and all your flowers and all your leaves
and all your cattle and sheep
won't match the riches that she receives
when for love she has made me weep

Wind River O Wind River
tonight I pray to my stars
Wind River O Wind River
she'll heal every one of my scars
and all your people and all your ghosts
and all the groans of the slain
won't match the face of her heavenly hosts
or the print of her love on my brain

STAYING WITH THE LAUGHLINS, JACKSON, WYOMING

Nearly twenty at breakfast
hair like sheet gold
I feel I know the place of children in this land

Say they finish eating at eight
at eight and some they have exploded all over
miles away from each other

the butterflies explode in gold air
fields broad enough to receive them all with wide
wide arms   and the fields enfold them

Rousseau's *Guerre* rides a Black with hair flying
the smallest has a cast in one eye   a gravel voice
she sits that Chestnut as if the pea sat the princess

Laughlin and I spend the day looking for trout
pools I shall never use   bird-man myself
long moments working water pieces

Later ''I think we may see moose along the Snake''
Laughlin says   I think I have a new joke about ''meese''
''I have seen moose every time up the Snake''

The Snake is a very fast river with silver tresses
drowns men in her hair   and patient pines
a porcupine lumbers out and disdains our wheels

There are no moose anywhere but L. stays calm
casting for fish in the Snake's foaming hair
while the hawks work like crossbows in the sky

As darkness falls two hulks rise from the river bed

50

"The father and his daughter the meese" L. says politely
the shape more impressive than the details of moose

which I never saw in the end on those shingles
In the light which would not go down the bats hunted
the mosquitoes gathered   busy on hand and arm

it seemed to me I knew precisely where I would die

CONNIE BURROWS, VANCOUVER ISLAND, B.C.

You—Connie Burrows
raised on Vancouver Island   western side
cried on the bus Victoria-Nanaimo
and on as far as Campbell River
I hadn't time enough
            for you to grant that coast

  I write to say I saw it in your dreams

''Our way of life is ebbing
the 27 mile beach taken over by surfers
Hell's Harriers they call themselves
the Americans come   with their own gas
they buy nothing from this land
they discover the Indian sepulchres
where the old poles crumble
cart them off to Seattle and San Francisco
in their groggy sea-planes
The Chiefs I know would make you welcome
with a week to spare you could make that coast.''

''There was the day the wild canaries migrated
damp clogged the wings of the hapless creatures
they fell in heaps all over our decks
the sailors carried the birds into their bunks
crying while they tried to warm them
but they all died
There was the day of the five ton sea-cow
basking in the sun
we heard the roar you can only call it a roar
of the killer whales
we got out of the way''

''We have picked up and let jobs fall
we go back to salmon time after time
I do the electronics
you can reckon on thirty losses a year
with the people aboard
Once we set out for the States
but we looked at each other
He said Connie let's go home
we have nothing to do in America
Once he worked in Alaska on the caterpillars
I fell ill and saw a freighter on the ice''

    ''He said Connie you have been so good
      I want to get you something
      I see myself walking thru grass back home
      with a black puppy beside me I said''

''The dog learned to bark as the fish pulled
he learned to swim among the porpoises
I could introduce you to every Chief
he was killed the black dog
I wanted to give up there and then
the killer whales tossed him up into the sky
tore him to pieces   all five tons of him
You have to keep one hand for the sea
one for the boat   one for your life
I fell and broke three ribs
You would meet with the warmest welcome''

    ''We'll go back to salmon in a little while
      get a better boat   I'll do the electronics
      our young ones are married   all stowed away
      you should really come out to British Columbia''

    The graveyard of the Pacific
    is battered by an ocean I've only seen much further south
    with waves above my head as I stood
    many years ago on the shores of Guatemala
    I believe the west coast of Vancouver Island

to be beautiful beyond description   ·
(tho the lives of Nootka & white are ebbing)
yet must satisfy myself with having been near it
It is recorded by de Fuca   Indians   Vancouver himself
it'll wait for me to see it on subsequent travels
there's no harm in leaving a corner unseen

but for you I write to say I saw it in your dreams

THE CRANES

for Kenneth White

The long white line alights
       cutting the trees
the core of the bird is not there
       lost against snow
the black wing-margins only
       bring in the night

this ground   pitted by war
       broken by ploughs
and scarred by harvest
       strewn under snow
with all earth's sorrows
       their dancing-place

a loping   flighting walk
       the undulating neck
beak spiked in mud
       and ceremonial screams
love white on white
       black lashes

her legs over my face
       flight on the drowned
the single rudder
       oil spill
into my eyes
       into my mouth

a year gone by without sound
       snow prints
of countless feet
       they lope thru trees

their legs whip back
      the long line stretches out and goes
unbelievably large
            cloud-weight on air
to populate the corners of the earth
            migrating to the moon   perhaps
their far
            unfathomable summers

rare jewels
            dwindling
mined out of all proportion to their yield
            her hull
after the flight
            settling the surface of my deeps

      in eternity I remember the birds

THE BEACHES

Twenty seven miles of beach you say
                    completely empty
white as a bone
                    in Baja California

well we would stain them only a little
we would walk up and down them first   back and forth
marking the place as ours   planting   so to speak
                    the banners

and then rest

but when it came to the point
the stain we'd make on that white wd. be a small stain only
the kind of stain in one place
                    humans make

                    in love   in love   in love

we'd wear woollen bathing suits to begin with
I'd strain the sea out of your suit with my lips
touch you at length thru the wet suit and smell
the tang of your coming thru the suit

                    and perhaps a little blood

                    and perhaps a little wine

would rot the sand as a sign of our passing

then we'd take in the ponderosa pines if there are such
as I like to think there are   taking that beach in their arms
and we wouldn't know for long our arms from the branches

our hearts from the birds   the red birds I imagine in the branches

there'd be a seaplane

to take us to other beaches

where we'd do the same day after day

in love   in love   in love

how we deserve those beaches

THINKING HER NAME

for M.S.

I have thought her name
in vacant corridors
along the walls of fake Greek temples
''Palladian'' porticos

in the offices with blind windows
where faculty abides
blind to a man behind blind windows
masturbating minds

In a soda-fountain   nineteen-nineteen
the oldest room in town
by oval candy-stalls I thought of Europe
old roses in her yards

and the new roses in her beds
that go by the name of July
and the shouting indoors
in an accent I'm rapidly losing

Where is the mind if you please
where is the erudition
the history carries this stare of youth
beyond the first semester of their eyes

I am bought for knowledge
they cannot use
old eyes going blind at their stations
cannot transmit by heart

Along all these I've thought her name
great body passing thru the air

with the gait of a giantess
you know that Baudelaire

and all the lovers she could have had
taking apart the poem of her name
looking for keys   breaking their minds
against the knowledge she is famous for

where I'd give all my method for her arms

AIRLINE FOR ARIADNE

for M.S.

In her tea-caddy land   five hours from here
she sleeps her measured sleep
and goes to waste like the earth
                    at season-break

I have found my rock
boats drive like snow across the sea
white bees in their ocean hive
disturbed by altitude

and I have the great cities eating out of my hand
at her bequest   and the rivers roll to my eye
the glaciers crawl   as on a moon
across my body

All this I have done for love
have done   for love
while she goes to waste like the earth
                    with her young men

necklace about her neck   stones on her breast
the pockets of her day   her broken dreams
her ankles as she paces the streets
or sits in libraries

We have loved well   reaped our reward
the young have passed as thru a grove of trees
whispered their message in our ears
we have looked at them with stone eyes

but we have heard them

The breathing of this continent
the heave of fields and hills   the gait of rivers
the seamless passage from hour to hour
in the four quarters which none can measure

leaves like a taste on our tongue
a taste for travels
the ruins we visit together
our children hung about our necks   become invisible

but we have heard them

And I sucked at her breasts with a lover's mouth
that am no son to her   though she's my nurture
fell over myself between her thighs
while she parted to let me drink her sources

as far inside her as her minerals
her copper ovaries
whose work turns the earth in its orbits
while the adepts noised about us thru our trees

We have loved well   and this is our reward
time will stand still for us   and let us breathe

FIRST CARDINAL

for M.S.

Seas lie between us
   we no longer move
      no longer act
            no longer speak
directly to each other

     but gaze across blue wastes
we are   look   nothing else
       vision
sight-summed
         between two wastes

remember I asked
    when that blood would first dry
no   would first come together
    still liquid   bright because liquid
closed in some crystal
    some piece of sky
       whose walls would not obscure it

wondering where   how   exactly when
    (even the date)
such rare red vision
    like the blood in our eyes
our tears
    catch in what tree
what bush   what thicket
      clean
or traversed with branch and bramble
              or shadow-shot

well
at eleven one morning
   one very clear morning
            as I said to myself
what an excellent time for birds
   meaning
   more than hour   more than seasons
wrapped in a longing for you
            thus   out of all time
         or
entirely in all time

tnere opened song
            a song
very longing
            as who would say Spring is unknown
and here I name it
            would say
I strive
                     to summarize

and thru dark glasses
            looking straight up
dark glasses for the glare
            there was that relic
   baronly scarlet
            encyclopaedic sermon
viz. re the ''blood''

   breast
   touched with a sunburst
   crest
            too high to be seen above high
just the suggestion of
            face jet
black   princely eyes

then   as I circled
   trying to see the profile

parting the distances
   he sang again

plumb over seas between us

               locking these gazes

HER LOVER, MINE

for N.B.

I stood in rain   face pressed to bark
entered into the spirit of the tree
licked leaves as if they were tongues
one in particular as if it were yours

I took a lover with a strange name
very much like an angel in generosity
who opened her arms as if I were love
tho she suspected I had no change

where she lay I measured her landscape
my hands moved up and down her fields
I grazed in her belly
and drank in the creeks of her thighs

but in every fall I found your hollows
and as I entered any part of her found him there
who was entering you in the same way
at the other end of elsewhere

it rained on this side of the earth and on that
while everyone I knew was crying in my dreams
and the whole length of America was trembling

TO SALAMANCA

for N.B.

1. THE FLAG

While
    from out there
moon, I suppose
the flag   dark cloud
announcing tempests

      Here
pristine colors
    red & ransom blue
white star beginnings
on the suburbs in ribbons
      which never end

the robin-mad
   red puzzle of your body
chess
      entering
your flow of blood
   on the blue sheets
      those stars we never chose

2. CHATEAUBRIAND AT NIAGARA

Je vous indique, Monsieur
     disons ainsi
   l'espace
le temps qui brule
    you know, the burning time

White barns
  smell of sweet grass

and Heuretebise, misspelt, but here
  in Lackawanna
        selling like tires
the fires of Hamilton   over the lake
        inking the waters
            flames above the mills
        Blake yet to come

Elicottville
        the pretty little town
everyone fucking
        behind closed doors
            soon   Salamanca

Czechoslovakia
        the sticker said
had the good gun laws

3. SENECA NATION

Over the house
the whole State's traffic roars
  Mohawk   Eastern   Alleghany
some internationals

By the great river
Anselm   Josie   Jerry   Diane
  picking at sandwiches
the house an Indian sits in
picking his way between words
        so carefully
the house angeled by goldfinch
we'd first seen in the rain
running naked in the State Park

Iroquois   Six Nations
  the long house looks like your house
(one nation?)
  the walls are as long as roads
        no builder dreams of

THE THREAD AS BEFORE

Lying half sleeping

with jerking limbs
I travel with her

but cannot imitate
the rolling of the ship

where she set out
grass withered
flowers withered
the sun no longer warms

the end of joy

where once we measured out
our holy place
planted our bed
a field for harrows

larches pall in the wind
branches spring no song
from birds dozing among needles
there is no coming in   no going out

and we have told this story before
fly-blown and pitted
and sucked this gall before
gone back on its beginnings

beyond heart-bearing

from the world's ends
many ships sail
I wish them well
except the one she travels

no desire for her feet on this land
to match footsteps with her
this land cannot endure
contamination

let him bless her
keep her
give her peace
who finds it possible

for I cannot

THE SEVEN YEARS

for George Economou

I'll go
    I'll carry
yes   all the wood
     all seven years of it
to win her back

This is no world
  this is no center
I mean   without her
   who has no mouth
but where I breathe
     no thighs
but where I enter
       no arms
but where I carry

Gold let me tell you
  isn't what's lacking
no   not employment
    freedom of speech
remuneration in good hide
     deerskin apparel
food on some days
        that soup
of lentils was it

Angels descending
    making a show of it
long rituals all night
    preening their wings
smart at the gate

smiling sidelong
eyelashes beating

She sits at home
        embroidering
looks out the window
        to catch a glimpse of me
as I break wood
        as I break bread
as I break silence

And the stars *work* I tell you
    the planets work   singing a little
        the world goes round on its axis
the dog with his ghost on his back
        the swan in her bridal plumage
time with time on his hands
        his sickle

This one
    come ransom time
she'll value freedom
        more than this mound of wood
she'll value angeldom
        the white skirts of her country
more than my pants

That wood begins to weigh on me

        that soup to pall

THE TRAINS

for Jerome & Diane Rothenberg

Organ chimes in the night
   the great trains hover over my eyelids
I underlie   their destinations

      but the factual train
lies at Princeton Junction
      impeded in its passage
from where to where
      the tempo fails to specify

I buy myself an America in dreams I cannot find

   By day the great trains go
   chain after chain of mountains
   desert after desert
               no limit
   to their progress
            the sea   even
   no limit to their progress
               they enter

the sea

   and   like the sun
         come back up East to start again

while she
   lies somewhere on that track
as the plane rises, drifting north
   that summer day shall I ever forget
the sea come alive with snows
   all the boats flecking foam

73

the sun devours them and spits them out
   she is down there

well: not quite
      about to reach it:
where Conn. / N.Y.   shoulder to shoulder
      beget rows of young trees

    By day
America shrinks
       to small communities
hemmed in by local news
the natives speak small news on the radio
in original, embarrassed voices

come to my store
   buy my products
      always much reduced
         sales all the year round
           not only do you save
              but you might meet friends as well
            and have coffee
              afterwards

whole careers
   all collector's items
      open to people on a local basis
        small   limited fame
          pretense even at art
            local communications
             local taxes
                community dreams

Behind her eyes

(as the bombs fall
   thruout my childhood
reading Lincoln's bio
   Allen and Nevins / or

Nevins and Commager I think
memorizing these States)

and the movies

(Mrs Miniver Jr, dying in N.J.
instead of Surrey as she pretends
soldiers and girls
opting over and over for marriage
something behind in the event of death
buns in all ovens)

learning

dog and burger America by heart
Grandma Moses by heart
the primitive made harmless
tit-touch and score
while the great trains
chime in the night

until that's where I come from . . .

LADYLIKE

for Anselm and Josie Hollo

1.

The delight of
not knowing a moment from now
      what it will be like
when our cheeks touch
   and we plant
a star of statehood in each other's mouths

her name should be
   Pocahontas / Minnesota / Kitkitdizze
     but is only X
     the steppes, a shrew,
     the Empress of New Jersey?

no snakes about under the couch
   no apples in sight
and whatever's standing in the corridor
     has lost its flaming sword

but the old king
   lies in his sheets and shivers,
he's brought fresh flesh for warmth
   and he doesn't believe it

no one dies of love these days, X?
no one ever even falls into it
     flat on his vacant face?

it's hands you know
   soft as fountains
   lips, tongues, teeth in their cages
   skins with the strokes of water

76

I undo her braid
want to steal the Woolworth ribband of the tress
   in which a few hairs are trapped,
    she says she'll get me my own,
      her hair like laughing water
        and the fainting of daughters

I talk to her roomate by mistake
      from a Seventh Avenue phone
You have the prettiest eyes in the world
      but this is not Pocahontas
oh damn   wrong woman!

2.

She had made food
   but it didn't seem to me
food was the point
    and tho
her handling of the food was finished
    she left a leg of it

the fancy bred—
   yet not the haze of roses
     waltzes
     ladies in crinolines / the old dark wood
I borned into a century too late
     would now come out of it

   I from before my time,
   she of her time
   and gifting it like unpretentiously,
    casually
      and timing it to be
     most literal

a couch
   one might have had to grapple with
     had one departed from
   the strictly vertical,

it's
tough making love to a couch

there's no alternative
   (go West young man go West)
   to floors and grasses,
        earth,
   coverings of sand and river bottoms
     if you want to fly

or if you want to pretend
   branches are making love to you
   stalks opening you out
      for the sun's inspection
   a daisy at your navel
    birdwings at nipples
     a cloud in the small of your back

ladylike

3.

Her charming life
sits on America fair and square
as she looks out over N.Y.C.
barks as she laughs
     between her vampire teeth

What she sits on she says
is new as California
   and I believe it
but have now been
  Verrazano too many times and
Magellan and Columbus and Vancouver
  and stood on Darien over and over:
she should have new metal

when I came here as a child
I was surprised to see out of the windows

everyone's life as a jewel
   strung on night's necklace,
tonight I remember these epiphanies
   in the windows of her eyes
not Dupont, G.M., nor S.O. of N.J. makes
   any prettier

her dress suggests small breasts
   at least I think it does
in the fashion and
      I would like to
(anointing my palms with oil)
   shine them for minutes
until I could see in their coins
    my presidency

she has come off the belt
   untold number of times
and yet she is of the line of Sheba
   and her foundation is Jerusalem's,
I thought at first I'd lost my maps
    but I've found in my old world
   the shapes news makes at night

apples for teachers
and other fruit
   her charmed virginity
   smelling of lilac and bruises
    o little heart
these great queens here look out on your princess
   saying welcome
with a bonnet of eagle feathers and dog teeth

THE OPPOSING COASTS

for Hans ten Berge

I have moved today
from jays to goldfinches and down again to jays
in memoriam olson and jeffers
        standing trees both
in the sharp smell of peppers

           the fatherhood
of these opposing coasts
        their leadership
  breaks me from sorrow
brings me from pain up to the vertical

old dryads in the trees
arms high above their heads
breasts cupped and tight
fine line of rib
    navel where the third lip
should rightly be
  flame at the gates of hair

la vida: a forest
(*no entiende*)
in each tree a poem
washed from the lover's loins
        into the standing air
        this month of bitter days
          with its polluted roots

and the hands
      upwards
        in a thousand branches
      everything rising

climbing
          except one bridge
one eye downcast
                    receiving the bridge

gone from that river   from that slide
turned from that birthing of me,
                    air, water, earth,
everything whispered into another ear
                    tongue lapping out at last

fire's upward lunge from this despair!

THOSE IN WASHINGTON

for Roberto Sanesi

Out breakfastless, at dawn, for warblers
    Virtue
         of
               solitude
        acute perfume:
  pines and anticipation!

Spring come round again—familiar
                resurrection.
Scatter of music.
The tanager flames from his tree-top
       the grosbeak weeps with his breast
victory fires.

        And from tree to tree
quick as needles
      almost invisible
    the little people / pygmies / the jewels
      of the world of air.

American redstart dressed in fire and mourning,
      cool, elegant, the black and white
      in stripes and spats,
perhaps the blackthroateds, but not certain,
      one with a back of sky
I've chased so long and never found—

      so high
     so high in the trees
   it is as if the wind had cried
     his words had   settled there
still beating like hearts in the branches

82

and violence of song!
destruction of all we build
in that many-throated passion!
the towers tumbled / walls
                    fallen to rubble in that song!

her hair
    woven with wings as with jewels
            a radiance in her eyes as of bright feathers
              in the quiet wood
    her body
            a tunnel in which the jewels leap like flames
                along the trees of its sides
            thru which I go   deaf to all but the music
                    and those falling cities

                I no longer desire . . .

SIN ALTERNATIVA

for George Buchanan

I am so thick that this world's problems,
the material problems refuse to go thru me,
stick to my hands like flies to walls,
like men white as the walls with hunger
and my skin also they refuse to leave
buzzing close to the skin longer than you would ever
believe they could endure the swatting.

I am beginning to understand how it is possible
for people in the very prime of age
to look forward to a long
uninterrupted sleep. Day wears from morning
until evening, down, and you fall
gratefully into the arms of your bed
and if there is someone in them you hardly notice.

Those who are weavers of light
cling tenaciously to this world and allow
the light to come thru their skins in such a way
that only the moral problems wear them down.
But these bring also the ever-restless guilts.
You would think that the vulture eventually
might finish his piece of liver
or that the rat would come to an end of gnawing
his sliver of intestine.
Nor does this happen either.

For those who continue to wish to work down here,
life has to provide some means of ending.
It switches the powers off one by one:
our needs, the joy one takes in them.
Eventually most of the things that have pleasured us

are wearied by rubbing away
or deadness of desire in the marrow.

Then we lie down and prepare ourselves
to be transformed completely into light
in order that we might be devoured by no other life.

ANNIVERSARY: IN A LYRIC'S MARGIN

for C.S.

"Voilà que j'ai touché l'automne des idées"

I have closed the door behind me
the Spring left *en couvade* outside
to break with tomorrow's birds.
    I am so much in love with the silence now,
more than with any woman: your doing.
No blame: your battle likes me well enough
    but we're allowed our temper.

O my beloved, (wonderful) things
left behind in another life!
          America, then?
was it to be / America then / the new life,
    —fall from the nest—
I'd gone to, losing my things to forgetfulness,
another's avarice, a stranger's cunning?

What was it I said to you,
Carla de Artemision,
when you began   imagination's feast:
         "I cannot hear
      but the silence has heard
         and now
    it is here, IN YOUR NAME"?

And they-all saying:
        the feminine is exhausted,
but it is just about to be carried
        around inside me,
mirror at last   answering back,
in this love of the mother silence,

86

and,   so deeply,   responsible!
              I would contend:
Wisdom is beauty / Beauty wisdom
but it would tempt lit. crit.
Heard a major singer among birds today:
his voice burst out with the authority of art
among the other singers   ipseity, the miracle in short.
Woman: Thing: Voice: O the possessed

draining away from me into the greening blades!
   Certainly
the most distanced confessional statement
              is the wisdom statement,
for the whole silent paradigm,
the generating Spring of this world,
everything that has gravitated up to that wisdom

is now behind it,   unspoken,   in my name.

OLVIDO INOLVIDABLE

for Octavio Paz

The suns of all the galaxies shine suddenly together
the world's blood unfreezes and
runs thru the forest of our veins,
we go with dream-ease thru all our recognitions
she had looked for me a long time between the snows
with the darts of the Arrow-bearer,
I have drunk of her blood at the source
and eaten of her amber load
and washed in the scald of her tears,
she is someone you know and have not seen for a while
you will see her again soon
because her time is wedding to my time
and we move everywhere in step together,
she makes gold in the daytime
and at night she mints silver
under her feet as she comes the dawn grasses grow,
she draws the great bow of our life
the arrow flies straight for the mark and hits heart,
she has found me again after much travail,
the forest is open again, the deer leap,
the hounds belt baying like mad water,
sun and moon wake in each other's arms surprised
and the stars make music together incessantly.

iv.xxv.lxxii. 05.00

STILL LOVE, WITH REPUBLIC

for L.W.

1.

No joy without guilt.
I dredge up from my life
all the dead at my hands,
the half-live, still in pain,
the fully-live,
        fresh in hope as at first,
wake from all these names of my sleep,
        light on your meaning.

No joy without fear.
I would I were to help you with your fears,
carry you thru them, take you
from the old century into the new
with all your qualities intact.
Apply you to my veins with your cool mouth,
my eyes with your snow-veiled eyes,
my sex with your mothering dark.

Brave, you are brave, with inner light
projecting to the world, in ink and milk,
and sometimes in the marvel of her colors,
the outline of your womb, a moving limit.

And in the depths of it, each other's darkness.
And on the edge of it, each other's light.

2.

The light has decided
buried after long years in her own husks
to pierce thru the world's protection

and bathe herself in danger,
flow out to her limit,
engage her maidenhead to the root,
leave no corner of the nether land in darkness.
She is like a sky that has eaten too many stars.

The male earth floods
        —lung's lake of tenderness
shot with blood and milk:
his brides bear apples and children
as if the light had mothered them thru him,
    he feels the weight of his responsibilities,
holds the doors in the sky open for her,
    courtesy becomes the form of all action:
        his arms around her knees
            sucks at her wherever he can,
                falls up to her, devours her.

He directs her flood,
downward towards him she swims,
lit by her own brightness,
        her eyes fall on his eyes,
her mouth drowns in his mouth,
        for him: a dream, as if climbing
                high over tongue,
as if, in dream, at last, speech . . .

3.

This morning you look at me out of the photographs
I took of you when you were happy
                wearing your shirt of earth.
I have made you, with your own craft,
                fairest in the land:
you are compatible with me your letter says,
                in this poem right here
let us confirm it.
Very suddenly there is little else
than neck in hands and slant of head

90

over my shoulder, reading this perhaps,
the glamor hidden in your workaday face,
the light you play with in your inner eye,
    your body's slope in the dark.
You are infinitely touching, you move me as you say
that I move you—a voice on which planes fly,
      far ships take water.
    I have made you long in the pictures,
tall, supple, long neck a sapling from your body's earth,
    cool breasts like fledgelings in a nest,
a curl catching your teeth on one side like a folded wing.
I want to fuck you as if the night was to end forever.
Now you turn your smile in on yourself, study your linings,
there is nothing lovelier in your eyes than the bewilderment
at this arrival of joy   who made it   we must have made it
      this instancy.

4.

I hang by fingernails
from your absence.
    Sharp pain   breaks
me in two: the weight you are in me
(a pregnancy around the heart)
must be distributed again, the weight
    shifted and balanced.
Darkness follows light in the room
levelled by illness. One moment I lie
bathed in a sea of light, the leaves
green mirrors on the grass outside my window,
next branches groan, and black
like ink in dreams, I write the night on you.
    I have been passing,
as is my custom, in and out of space,
today from Avila to Santa Fe,
I study where you are in Santa Fe,
bite in and out of knowledges like fruit
    among mind's leaves.
    Work season's over,

mower, my animal, sleeps in the fireplace,
stabled down there for the capriciousness
of his defaulting motor. The light you loved,
dallies with you in all my photographs,
smoked Pennsylvania light, plays on his flanks
webbed by the spiders. Time to make food, and soon,
tonight, your picture waking me among the pills,
I'll follow you about the reaches of this country,
accept with joy your own America: why should I not,
taking with me so much, take the wide-wayed as well
belly of land, your own thick navel-belt,
sandwiched between the mountains and the sea?
    Sleep. Far below
you straddle the sun's sleep, travel huge steps,
your knees like clouds in the Midwestern sky.
And I
      fall thru your legs to find a homestead
fall thru your thighs to be reborn.

5.

How quiet our days, in contrast to all else!
The President falls from the stars
down to the barber-pole of this Republic
with all his busy-boys bustling below.
The country is one long AH! of astonishment.
    I am in New Hope, Pa.,
and you in Santa Fe, N.M. Red leaves and sand.
Bare branches, snow. This morning gives clear skies
    to both our faiths.
    Creaking towards a birthday
we know love is America to us, old land and newfoundland,
and waits some Spring, godknows, if it can find it.
We know, as the sap rises, we should call
Adams and Jefferson, Thoreau and Melville down
and young Walt Whitman back to rotting Camden.
Our sweats outbuy the dollar any day.
    You and I
for different but equivalent reasons,

92

are the last two on earth to believe in
    manifest destiny:
we would like our poem to tell
tourists in New Hope and in Santa Fe
something else about our ageing country than bargains.
Now once upon America shall we hold hands
as if we were two coasts with the whole land between?
Reform the morals shall we?
Hand in hand, your name and mine, we wander into time
as you shall picture me, so shall I sing your beauty!

6.

Spending evenings alone   giving thanks for
    the miracle of being
what we have wanted to be all our lives
when we would have been more likely
to fall with the rest of mankind—
we can share it together,
    I can say:
over there she meditates on my divine essence
while I, over here
    meditate on hers—
and a turbulence in the light
announces a novel couple
    in the annals of love.
    This is a time in which,
for technical reasons of high import,
    we are obliged to write very complicated poems.
    I write my share of such
    and reap my just deserts in selling too few books.
    It is pleasant to think
that it is also possible to write simple poems
    remembering the girth of youth's ambition,
the satisfactions of mid-career
    and the changelessness of the human shape
        by and large.
                            Let the light
be beautiful above, below, and all around us

as the people say where you now are
and as we touch each other, so shall we touch ourselves:
and as ourselves, so shall we touch each other.
                              Meanwhile the Republic,
as we go about this pregnant business,
   and the government collapses
the Republic for the moment can go hang.

THREE COMINGS TO THE HOUSE OF LEAVES

for M.S.

One

This house, surrounded by leaves
    like a ship wrapped in surf,
this house we'll call the house of leaves as long as we live,
    the sail of triumph—

New Jersey August,
    aquarium haze,
    shadows piling up behind each other, rain-jungles
    in the far trees
and then sharp against the wall of distance
    a fear that nothing will hold—

    Half-naked on the terrace,
    sipping tea,
    the desk squared yet again, papers set straight,
    pencils contained in jars, the mail sorted
    a thousandth time: the mail sorted
    beyond all need to do so / I know well / . . . and
                           bathed
in our bodily signal of lime-flowers
    the smell on my skin like your touch

each leaf in meditation
                all by itself
forgotten the other leaves on the branch,
          on the other branches, the other trees,
                   repose begins,

six years we've labored (near seven at this writing)
—counting the last few days of seventh as our rest—

you come at last into some sort of repose
in the obsessive poem weaving your arrival
                    a meditation of joy achieved,
and the house furnished with joy as with chairs,
beds, tables, desks and bookcases
and the cooking of fine foods, aromatic on leaves,
                    and of our bedding down together:

   no need to go   no need to go   no need to go

                    the house awaiting our sails
like a still clipper on the surf of leaves . . .

Two

From branch to branch, arrow to wound,
tree top to bottom like a cascade,
almost a somersault you'd think, astounding speed,
circling sometimes like racers round a post,
                    birds at their feeding.

The birds as a record of my life's tracks
the recording of the birds eventually *is* my life
and the punctuation of my work as I stop to watch them:
breaths between one breakdown and another:

   If one were to take away these tracks
as daemons might suddenly be taken away
   by the advent of a high god
or politicians be swept under the carpet
   by a dictator
ah the terror at being suddenly left alone in this existence
   like a bleaching bone!

You come to the house of leaves, you arrive,
and the tracks change direction.
                    No longer
from myself to myself only the short day

long with work only, but short on breath and freedom,
but from myself to you, the weaving of paths,
goal of exertion—if there be any goal in this life

making of food and bringing it out on platters,
preparation of anecdotes for entertainment,
smiling dictations of knowledge shared,
ah the lists, and heraldries of days in love!

                    And the meanings,
acquired by every moment, the secondary layers
of meaning which take off from the first, and the first
having no value apart from the second
                             which is you here.

Three

Leaf on leaf   branch on branch   leaf behind leaf
branch interleaved with branch
                       pages open on air
green layers going back into the wall
                       of distances I don't explore
wishing to be bound in
                    enwombed
in a lining of leaves with delicate veins, like hands
closing me into silence,
                   profoundly embedded,

and the life among leaves
the bird appearing as a distant shadow, colorless,
remaining a shadow: I won't see him, ever again,
and the bird, caught between leaves, part of him in shadow,
part of him caught by light
                  and granted color ╱ or the bird
close-up in the closest trees, presented on the branch,
almost with a label on him so clear his livery,
like a flag, a banner of the material universe,
                  one of the names of God:

So: held in the layers of the mind, your various repose
facets of body I love, some light, some dark,
standing in the far trees and coming gradually into the light
                as the leaves fall
and the waiting is on, for you to come out of the trees
out of all the dead days of our lives
                for you to come to hand
out of thought, out of remembrance,
the tangibility of your defects
                as perfect as your perfections . . .

                first in my outer arms,
in the remembrance my arms have of you, relived again,
all the times we made love gone thru again—
compulsive repetitions—
                and the slow recognition
the coming forward into inner arms, center of love,
our reality fucked at last, exhausted,
                and unpursuing,   unpursued,
the light stealing out of our eyes,
                to the farthest trees . . .

FOUR
FOUR
FOUR
FOUR
FOUR
FOUR
FOUR
FOUR
FOUR
FOUR
FOUR
FOUR
FOUR
FOUR
FOUR
FOUR
FOUR
FOUR
FOUR
FOUR
FOUR
FOUR
FOUR
FOUR
FOUR
FOUR
FOURFOUR
FOUR
FOUR
FOUR
FOUR
FOUR
FOUR
FOUR
FOUR
FOUR
FOUR

TO MELTZER AT BOLINAS, A COMMISSION RE S.Y.

And where is the alphabet of creation in the names of the fifty states
and why is the white horse running thru the halls of the academy riderless
and why does she have her middle fingers on my nipples while reciting aleph
and why did the flag flap so strongly in the breeze in my thirty third year

    that is Babylon in her eyes in the name of power and of equilibrium
    amen?

Maybe I sat in the house wrapped in white with black stripes in my eyes vertical.
And black stripes across my belly: the stars blood-red.
And made myself comfortable and gave the vegetable earth enjoyment with grasses
while a great smoke came out of her thighs that I inhaled as I drank her love-juice.

    She is wrapped in frost because she has brought the crab into evil
    ways in his ascendance and his home.

Shall say wisdom. I do not think you shall. Not yet at any rate. Not here and now.
But it came to this, on Washington's Birthday, the masters said efface, efface, efface.
On the threshold of summer—you know: like, split. All the conditions for baking Jerusalem:
all those old recipes for the cooking up of Heaven in the New World.

    I remember the stars and stripes rising in value up the sky with
    Taurus in the ascendant and my head hurts.

But snake. Snake dangling from the roofbeam of the house and ready to go in.
That in the bowers of the Rockies, that in the deserts of Nevada, that in the cas-
cades of Wyoming I should take her great paps and have suck . . . . yes and
have suck of that great wisdom of the old they call this life / this death.

    He took her in the Sabbath of his mouth and named her tenderly and said
    I love you.

God of Greeks! While they continue to hold the great sale of lyrics and flutes
and all the harps they had hung up in the trees went for very little
and would not even fetch the price of an old Impala or a Thunderbird
at the Washington sale or the Lincoln sale or the Kennedy sale if it came to that.

    She said it's a pity you have no language and have become an
    intercontinental bum. Thou restless shift in peace.

Dey watch while I adjusted to de new requirements and de letters in my voice
began to slur and I enjoyed de wind in my voice as one with an Eagle Pass

to all de national parks in de West including de Grandy Canyon.
And dey said dat dis vas an interesting phenomenon Tarn going all Atlantic.

And why can't I make up the mind of my life for God's sake
and stop living alone in this kitchen? War on wisdom is my bane today.

Called my moon and my saturn all the way over to her saggitarius and asked
what is it that made you such a killer of forms in Babylon that day baby
made you efface all those beginnings for my mind and start again without form
and she singing like Flack the other night, you know, that close, and un-dressing . . .

She split her sunny cornucopia for him and he looked deep inside
where it parted.

Perhaps the elk lay down. The buffalo lay down. The deer lay down.
I have it from a farmer in Santa Fe whose hair is as long as the wind.
And who has sat in his house wrapped in a white shawl and waited for letters to move
gracefully gracefully O Israel hear and behold hear and behold your countrymen

because Aphrodite is near to thee and carries her babe on her back
and they call her squaw and it papoose.

Rather long ago when men juggled, they cut up other men to find the soul inside
and if there was no soul inside they said that these were the lost tribes of Is.
And you wouldn't imagine what went on in these States and beyond them all the way down
to the South. The message flew up and down on winged sandals between Salt Lake and Teotihu

O my grace. I thrash about with you in midnight play. And then
light the ashes of sweet odors.

Tears sold the land. Tears sold the house. I sold my tears and their source.
And I sold the longing wind behind me that carried the noise of grasses to my ears.
Its name had the syllables of Babylon and it ruled all the sounds of the harp
when the moon shone over our days of exile and we grovelled on the long marches.

My servant is in my bath and his heart is full of gin and blood rises
into the gullet of my womb and I smell.

Hey she can't extradite me from New Jersey the Queen of Manhattan no she can't
even tho she thinks mistakenly that I can't see women because I'm blind about them
but you know that flower of a girl makes up her mind about stone and that's the shine
it has all day and every day from the creation to independence . . .

and that's why I'm going to have to ram this banner and strikes
down her throat until I'm green in the liver from b.o. eighty.

Which is to say that our external services have picked up colonies in all known lands
and that the farthest are about the farthest that any human being could have gone.

102

And we have said each time this is ours. Bully bile in the desert. Basta. Enough.
I will not wander in the desert one moment longer living a mile from my neighbor.

She, Martha Washington, saying that from a pip will spring a
cranberry bush in the very bogs of the Jersey.

Zere will never be anozer time like it. Twins. Gable and Mrs. Miniver. Canyon & Cindy-Jo.
I will have ze American pellicula under my shawl as perfumed as when it came from ze box.
I admire Cornell. And Jess and Johns and Dine & Rivers. And Stellassippi too.
Ze savage meanings of ze earth, where ze geese step, and Labrador's in sight.

But she took on the name of Miriam. Rosemary R. Lynette of the first
kiss. And Ruth the gory balls. The lay whose name's forgotten.

Hours. Thirteen blue hours over Shannon gone below and it cd. have been to these poor
oh all these tired and poor in a row in nineteen forty two and not a second later
giving me time to dip into the language and loose my silence and loose my innocence
ah all those forms gone like smoke up winter chimneys in the island homes

knitting an Aran sweater on Block Island: drowned she said,
I nearly drowned in fourteen footers. But got out sideways.

The constitution fades from my mind. It had not been there. The Declaration of Independence
fades from my mind. It had not been there. The Lion's gossip too.
In New Rochelle. The Constitution of the Supreme Court of the United States and
whatever documents they have about the feeding patterns of the Army and the Police.

It was in Cuba that she turned up as the only funnygirl policeman
and it was a pistol woman not a modess.

Yah! the ending of the forms. Because of the transposition of the imagination,
growing hot in the pressure cooker like a badly packed joint and driving out
every inch of this lousy-sell-and-be-damned culture and poisoner of minds
in Illinois of the Illinois and Minnesota of the Minnesotas.

She was the Statue of Liberty with her own torchupherass
quenching herself in the harbor.

Love be thou ready at this moment consciously to choose death, then thou shalt know
that thou hast come far enough to receive the influx as she sits on your knees
and be filled with awe of the Shekinah which is near thee
before the undressing of the great land: when her clothes are thrown into the balance.

And she said: I will give you Connecticut and the Carolinas
and in dowry thou shalt have Arizona and L.A.

Noon of the Prince. Which is Prince—as that Third George, or better still, Henry V.
Come now the grey rain and the cotton rain and the black rain of Vancouver,

come down the peace of the sweet sleet that covers Washington and Oregon in winter,
and down the bull I saw stand in a shower of gold coming from the air about him:

> for she had that green thing in her eyes as she walked and her fingers
> were scorpions asleep.

So she goes into the Rockies burning with anger and exits peacefully on the other side
having roamed away her childhood as a centaur, half human half beast,
and pierced the mountain lion with the arrow of her right hand to bring down Babylon
and torn out his liver and sent it to the Presidency of the United States

> and I have peace from her eyes in the month of Kislev because she is
> the mirror of the Sun of my perfections.

Aphrodite of the laughters brings in a tethered goat to the feast and he goes
beh, beh in the language Texan. I heard saccharine for sourcream in the language Texan.
The Dragon king on his throne, the king in his city, the heart like a king at war:
all fall from these three by mysterious paths that lead from the peaks to our valleys.

> Her hands on my hands like hands against a mirror and the truth in
> the midst of them: This is the Place of the World but the World is not
> Its Place.

Ts ts ts. Calling the warblers down. Ts ts ts. Man blood and woman blood in their feathers
Father and Mother of all created things in their belly of sand. Walking in beauty.
It is walking in beauty down the mountains pouring birdsong like water down the mist's sides.
The right foot on Colorado, thinking; the left foot about to drop on Utah, ah forgetfullness!

> No, no, it is warm in her heart between her tits in Jerusalem. Rothen-
> berg? No, Tarn. Breton passe, et le reste.

Query the letters shining from inside like the gardens I dreamed of as a child.
I said: the garden will consume itself in its own light, not burn away.
And the fish in the pools will not be cindered but fly about like happy birds.
The letters assemble in groves and migrate to their sleeps. As they close their eyes they rush out
and return

> Giant columns backed out of an air no one can grasp.
> She is beginning to mean the sum of her perfections (33 / 33 / 33).
> In her eyes is the Sun going West.

THE FORMULAE

One

He has attached the crowns to the various manifestations and they have each said Ego.
Eye guarantee this and that and take out your left kidney in a wink.
Lillith. Eve. The great one, the really big one of Babylon—nothing less.
Like astronomical salaries. Weekends on Hawaii. Personal IBM's. And tenure.

Two

The conditions of the East and the conditions of the West and the great silk routes
When they saw the Star it was too late: the dispensation had been for ever and ever
Blessed be He. She is the Lady of such and such a Hand and she takes that Hand
and passes it ever so gently over my cock like a wind out of Tiflis.

Three

Great Fathers I am among you but if I forgive not a word, forgive me. Open sky.
Open house of my fathers, take me unto your bosoms masters of this world and I will teach
great mandalas. The world is a cube, is a square, is a circle, is a sphere.
Ah, sweet intellection: how ravished I am by thy members. Three to poke, one to go.

Four

Oh God, not all the numbers! He is sitting on the heights of the World
and from him as from a canopy depends the whole of creation, Blessed be He.
And even the serpent falls from his tail, its maw into the abyss,
downwards, downwards, far past Taurus and Aries and all the angry animals.

Five

A tangerine canary saying more or less: yes, the color of evening. And his mate:
no, the color of morning, and you have to tell where it's at by the colors.
By sheer bravado. By sheer ullullet, and rigoror, and krakula.
The shawls of the Fallen Kings drifting down and down into the Ocean.

Six

She told me she was immersed in the Ages and that by and by it would pass.
She said she envisioned taking the great structure to pieces and showing just how
it made her come most magically by rubbing the shaft to the right as the just may do.
I say: in thy lips are marvels and in thy tongue I find the measure of all deeps.

Seven

And for the first time I have transformed myself into Chance. I have put it about
that my prick which wants the running comfort of her philosophy

declines the sale of the Virgin Islands to the Middle Kingdom because of pollution
and the havoc it is supposed to cause at West Point. I said leaves and there were.

Eight

It is too long ago to remember if anything was said (or not) about her sweet lips.
I know that they part a little like the beak of a Western tanager
we found on the road in Montana once and buried its gold and scarlet banners.
I'll spend all of my life trying to sound her name.

Nine

It took a very long time before I could reach the understanding of comfort and dig
the slow smile that spread to my lips as the evening wore on and I fainted
some seventy-two times in a row and finally believed in the evidence of my own eyes
to come up perfect enough to find fault with myself and face ONE.

Ten

Whom I had not known. Selah and Great Seal of the Commonwealth of Nova Caesarea.
Whom I had not known, nor heard spoken of, nor heard whispered about in the—
Trouble with this country he said curt and European; Oh those circumlocutions!
It has no language. Selah. It is perfectly contented and successful. Selah. It is dumb.

FIVE
FIVE
FIVE
FIVE
FIVE
FIVE
FIVE
FIVE
FIVE
FIVE
FIVE
FIVE
FIVE
FIVE
FIVE
FIVE
FIVE
FIVE
FIVE
FIVE
FIVE
FIVE
FIVE
FIVE
FIVE
FIVE
FIVEFIVE
FIVE
FIVE
FIVE
FIVE
FIVE
FIVE
FIVE
FIVE
FIVE
FIVE

THE FIRE POEM

for Janet Rodney

1. As Prologue

The fragility of Summer,
the belief it is never quite real
between two walls of Winter,
        but it burns now—

and after an age of nights
all I have to do is fall asleep tonight
        and tomorrow
reality will be her presence.

Reality will be—not her arms
but walking thru them to the clarity
of air behind her where her angel stands

        herself writ fire!

2.

Immortally beautiful
        as she passed
that day in the flame of her hair
        with the fast eyes of ships,
stopped Rome that day, stopped Athens,
        stopped, even, Jerusalem,
stopped woman's city whole
                        and FLARED
like a new culture,
        sail of her being ∕ over the rooftops
like a great pilgrimage
        the birds, the animals, the grasses
                        of the city

        saying (in new found voices)
this newfoundland:
look / she is going / in that flame of hair
        towards a furnace,
towards a revolution
        —immortal beauty—
there is no news of yet
                                in all these voices—
but news there will be. Soon. Soon.
                        After the night.

3.

And I would eat her
        if she were one great feast
of all the year's feedings in that one day /
    the dreadful season of regret
gone by, and overboard,
        and a new happiness
clean as night air
    over the soaking city,
cool as a shower
    over a body worn with work,
    as I would eat and drink fire,
venture my manhood into fire
        —all the hair singed—
—and the skin blackened—
        —the root exposed,
like a dead tree stump—
    if it meant breaking thru
to a new light.

4.

Nothing but the night, frankly,
        nothing, no nothing but the night—
as I have said many a time
        noche oscura del alma / y de la civilizacion
and then
        under the brink of a black hat

110

(felt, gypsy-like)
      the red face of the goddess
                androgynous a little,
breathing familiar fire over my tongue,
pouring the wine into my throat,
the molten gold
      a day of happiness distills—
the eyes like witches' eyes,
      like two live coals
from her leather country,
      the teeth like childrens' bones
or the bones of birds—white, white
                and the smile sailing,
surf on an unknown sea with a dawn rim
              on the day of discovery

5.

Asking myself why
      I had frequented that beauty for so long
without discovering
      that it was *major*—
      as one says of a poet,
      or of a goddess,
ever weighty affairs:
      the things of love, or fate, or history—
      that he or she is major,
asking myself why I had not before
      begged her to aid me
in these poor undertakings,
      these odysseys into the world below
bringing in kelp, or iron, or the flood
      of mercury in motion thru our lives
  (as she might, in a cloud of fire, or a pillar of same,
  unfurl a banner, say, or manifest
  a special friendship . . .),
telling her:
      now, you see, if you would come,
      we could—this continent—

name it, island by island, cape by cape,
mainland by mainland (corn and vine)
       city by city of devoted men:
we could name it together, and in no night,
      in no night would the names
   ever be lost,
      but it would take full day
and all the light of all the men who'd ever been, together,
      to drown it out,
and by *common* consent:

        Which is impossible . . .

6.

I had said to myself
   I needed her absence
in order (quote, unquote) to be ''in love''
   and to write poems
but had forgotten
   these were the days
       of a new life.
When the sun rose on that homing day
—curious: the sun and not the moon,
the matrilineal, lunging out of the East—
I had had fears
   the sweetness
would be exhausted too quickly—
       I had forgotten
these were the days / of a new life.
And if she were to spit blood on the earth
and drown it in her loss, a howling dragon,
in the remembrance of her imperfections,
still, there would be words
to describe her fullness now
   as she runs beside me (in the new life)
        unrecompensed / unheeding.

7.

To be happy like this day
   many days need to have been lived,
much coal needs to have been fired,
many beings to have informed that coal,
many fates to have woven those beings—
   to be rich like today
   with her stillness beside me
like a pulse in the blood, that homely a matter,
   yet how miraculous—
to have eaten as we ate today
   like kings at table,
and to have spent
   like princes lavishly comparing
the goodness of each earth the gods had gifted them—
  to be at peace now
with the energy spent
 and not in vain,
breeding, out of its ashes, energy again,
   many fires must have been set
   under the phoenix,
   much wood cut down
   to build the pyre,
   many great deeds performed by us together
   and many gifts of each one's life
   to beast or conqueror,
               or to each other,
   in a past almost too distant
   to bear the knowledge of
               with equanimity.

8.

How can,
   how CAN that noise,
that noise of fire, or noise of powered waters
   come from (from nothing) and from
so much silence?
Was poor.   Was starving.   The dead had said:

"Enough, oh and enough."
    "We have seen you too often".
And I had told them
    "Will pay you one more ransom"—
always one ransom,
each time more blood, more time, more prince's life.
Until I was afraid
I would not have enough
    —nor would there be enough
in the whole city—
    to ransom that dead one again,
to bring her up, silent and all-forgiving,
    like the sun from under the sea
by the stream's side
    back to snake's meadow.
(That word was strong, man, that word you said,
like that was weighty, man, in the clearing.)
The payment fell into the void, I weary.

And she rose up beside me, as if the mist were praying.

9.

I would have the stars
        bow down to her,
I would have the days
        take on her name
and be her namesakes,
        I would have the moon
sail thru the sky for her smile
        and hers alone,
having no other motion
        than in her pleasure,
I would have my words
        live and die on her lips
with no other function
        than to give her voice,
call her one day,
        saying "I've finished,

we can go to the great sky,
might as well start naming
        the land from there''.
I would simplify the word
        until she stood inside it,
the word incarnate,
        the only goddess.

BETWEEN DELAWARE AND HUDSON

"'All women are beautiful as they rise
exultant from the ruins they make of us"
—Robert Kelly

1. STALEMATE IN THE CITY

for T.N.

Call back all images.
The images called back.
Body of woman / squat generations.

Now that we have called back all images,
all visions of the future in these lineaments,
body of woman
          whom I have borrowed from time's looms
and will give back to time eventually,
          how shall we recognize
the splendor
          of our original and given faces,

and of our making hands—
the shapes we give to matter
          resistant in the night
to all our arts:
          the running glaze over our skins
and the onion of hope

where it peels off
our lesser clothes?

For the clothes of the spirit,
the presences that ride beside us,
          angels with cut-glass eyes,
judges of weight,
          waiting for the song to soar
over the body's waters.

The divine weather changes
inside the orbit of her eyes
          and the stars go mad.
She bends in the night elsewhere
          over her hands
strong in their processes:
          the frightened clay
recognizes its maker . . .

She leaves me asleep
among my best intentions
          poor as a city bum
unwashed, unloved,
          calling back images
for my immediate sake.
          Later she wakes me to the gold
wealth on her skin of clay—

and, as the dawn smelts our first ores,
her night, my day, fuse momentarily.

2. FIRST MOVEMENT, ON THE DELAWARE

Her right foot lifts the wind
as she leans upon it
       it presses into earth,
we go to bird together,
       she-falcon at my wrist,
below the revolutionary tower.

Under her wings as she flies
from my right wrist, the avenues of air
open to talon-tread
       and she has risen
height of a knee relaxing and unfolding
       into a flower of movement.

Streaking in liberation
across the wide divide—
       the space between her talons—
in wing-pits leaves unfurl,
the trees come to conclusions
       renting the light.

Moves the other foot sideways
putting down without weight
begins to shift the body to the lure
       of the next moment:

trap of the whole migration
her wingspread holds the birds,
they name their names in distant trees,
       the stream sings underneath.

and her hands, loose at the wrists,
taking their stance from mine

float up into the wind her talons make
      far ahead of her sight,

she draws in wings,
plummets to treetop, pinions bend
all summer in her taut embrace,
        bow of the mountains:

        Where is the arrow
as her hands fall through air
fingers trailing like feathers
or tails of butterflies—
colors like streams
        within the light?

In turn of time, in keeping,
tells me the names of all my battles.
Her hands have come to rest across my hands:
we prepare the next position.

3. THE BIRDS SUSTAIN HER

All the birds I do not know
        in marvelous solitude
her eyes inhabit,
all the birds I have seen in my dreams,
isolate splendors as in a color plate,
    imagining
        season after season
their plumage lastingly
    fixed, fallen, as if dead on ground,
        the dorsal Eden
seen from above—
especially the blue
    of sky, so faint, so pale
        of the Cerulean,
all this *sub specie*
            aeternitatis.

            The high tower
locked in its memories,
blind windows onto history now dead,
the Delaware in the arms of its fields,
the rain hugging the hill, a menace,
but also a peace, the rains will keep out men,
        very close to the eye
bird tropics rise from the far south
in clouds of sweat,
    jungle-born sun
runs like a glaze over strange skins:
        men of a dying past.

The tanager
burns in the gloom
in brackets of black wings,
    his coat the grenadier's

in some disbanded regiment.
His female is busier than he.
    As I turn in the cold to go,
the first inhabitants move through the woods,
  swift mocassins.
He hovers on his mate
  Delaware, Delaware,
three times before his sexing wearies.

All the birds I do know
comfort her as she cries—
this summer going from us as the passage blurs.

4. BLITHEWOOD ON HUDSON

Since he had said: let there be a poem,
(whose wide arms encompass the gate
         and whose world-body,
I suddenly remember,
belongs to the order that might be hers)
         let it be so:

in the octagonal room,
her washing done, she takes my starved
and therefore clumsy body into hers,
breaking the rim of habit—and I scream
with all the ghosts in the house,
running my fingers down
         her night-dew,

shudder again under her sleep . . .

Morning. The lawnmowers
power the gardens, the roses hum
that are stars somewhere in her keeping
and not yet out / the southern birds
mad with the north, careen around
daughters of Hudson sunning their backs,
formal gardens, fathomless lawns.

We wander thru my fatherhood of her,
everywhere she is taken for my daughter
that will not bond with birds,
that will not wing me from moment to moment
and recognize, so that I may remember
and heat in the gloom like a kiln
on our return,

shudder again under her waking . . .

122

And cannot marry her in any sense,
cannot assume her skin
under my hands,
Delaware, Delaware of the golden back:
father of wolfbane and mandrake,
she circumscribes my palsy.

Letting it be so:
the rooms are empty in the morning
and the memories empty.
I stifle under her sleep, wake and get up,
walk out beyond the city's curve

never more to see her in this life.

5. SECOND MOVEMENT, ON THE DELAWARE

She turns to the right
    bringing the bud of air
to easy flowering,
leans forward on the right, as if to fly,
    the left heel lifts:
she is so vulnerable

and saw her as a child
    for the first time
who had been such a woman to me,
    muse in starlight,
her nose in my affairs
up to the hilt,

saying: ''look at my beauty, my beauty,
the beauty I see in my hunger for this world''—
    but could see
only her own beauty, and not another's
only her hunger /
            protecting those wild foods.

Then: the internal wings
that speak to each other of great goodness given
mentioned that out of the mouths of sucklings
   —even she who had sucked at this manhood—
the path of their own stars and the era's stars
conjunct in time: out of these mouths
    our ends would come
unlooked for.

And we run, we dance, we fly around her
who are looking for the motionless wisdom
until her stillness gains us
    and move and stillness both

lapse into happiness.
> She lifts the left foot

extends it before her, the body gliding
to face the future fully
and she troubles us with a growth of wings,
an understanding around the head like an aura,
speaking to us in the tongues of silence,
the silence resounding in our skulls,
with the words we would know
> if we but voiced them . . .

Rise of the Spirit of Independence:
the tower this morning is weary,
the trees are full of bird noise
> but no birds.

I shall continue to prove us.

6. THE MIRROR, BACK IN THE CITY

The palm of her left hand
faces the palm of her right,
after the stranger is pushed away
    palm rests on palm:
still butterfly.
She flies the Delaware tower
back to the city.

My friend the dispossessed
talks thru the night
his defences falling,
one after another:
    ''I am poor,''
he admits at last:
''have not fucked in a year''

and the sadness sweats out
with his alcohol,
desperately he looks at
his interlocutor:
    ''Can you say
anything about that'' he asks,
at last, and the other will not.

He turns from his friend
looks down into the carpet,
under the floor to a ceiling,
thru the depth of a room
    to a bed
on which a mermaid swims
unconscious of his pain—

    the floor below
an ocean of drowned birds,

the thrashing fledgelings
hoarse with his misery,
but the two talking
talk well into the dawn
completely out of sleep,

''and I give you,'' he says,
''those who believe and those
who do not and cannot believe
for the world owes them no honor.
They are the caterpillars
that never make it into chrysalis,
let alone into butterfly.''

Immense and ever baffled longing
for the exact mirror of the heart:
the arms stretched out
giving ╱ receiving,
the mirror breaks,
and out into the heathen world
the poor hands grope and bleed . . .

7. MELUSINE, ON THE FLOOR BELOW

From the sky of her bunk,
her two feet coming towards my chest,
        balance of left and right
lost for a while,
        the thick thighs flash with scales:
"you have the shape of a mermaid,
        can you have children?"

"And are you bird or fish
laying warm eggs or cold
out of that marvelous dew?"
Laughing, (she'd not heard this before),
forgives for it a thousand sins.
And the wings go crazy in her eyes
        for a moment.

Melusine,
above the towers of the city
        as princes die,
on her left tail she swivels
and brings her fins up like wings.

"All week among the fairies:
I have not seen you. One day perhaps with you
I'll grant, but never lightly."
Delaware, Delaware: the coins
slide off the fish scales and take no hold.

The have nots and the haves
with no business together:
the migration is over,
the spring is gone into the wings;
all over summer:
the wanderers, lost at sea.

Her children are monstrous,
they burn each others' lives,
I break off her fish tail,
the night weeps in my hands,
she makes no love she's giving free:
          payment's the measure.

"How many lives shall I pay?" is the question,
"how many moments move into your stillness,
how many times give over my life to yours,
          in sacrifice,
with no response in your eyes?
Is there a chance" is the question
          "of response ever,
will you swim up ever   out of the sea?"

Now the moon enters into her dark quarter.

          It is her *caritas* that saves me.

8. MOVEMENT ITSELF

Kinesis—
    movement,
the pest
    keeping us in action,
forcing us
    beyond the momentary desire
into the invisible curve of our lives /
yet knowledge beyond that moment
        not clear in any reasoning,
(any more than the movement of armies
        to define a state,)
but in *collegium,* the total mind, o.k.

And the plunge of wings
        the guiding archangels
            of this era,
working (and with their immobilities)
        for the clarity of the state—
her voice droning away in the background
        among the voices of warblers,
her profile (eyes and nose covered with feathers)
            becoming brighter
as the tower rises above the hill,
carries each scale of its body
            into the light.

Kinesis
  of the holy stars across the firmament,
the movement of the profile
        turning, with no thought for the past,
her voice comes out of me with no bidding,
        my mouth as if between her thighs,
            —the bearded woman,

the breasted man, exploding cunt-cock—
  giving birth to the tower,

Working in another time
not in accordance with the time I'm given
           which is another's
and a prison /
                 I abdicate
to work in my own time
           like a bird flying—
the provision of food
           in the world's hands:
swallows on the Delaware bridge
           launched at the wind
and back to the bridge with their prey.

That my voice is not my own any more
has been becoming clearer for some time :
it comes out of, mark, out of
I know not what mouth, mouths, paramouths,
other entrance, door, gate or passage (of any sort)
           vulva or mouth,
  mark: out there in the world,
or within, before, very long ago,
or again, after and projected forward,
           like the swallow's incision,
twist: and a hole in time
           from which all comes to birth:

gate / gate / paragate / parasamgate
     matter, all hail
     wisdom, all hail—

Eyes of diamond. The look. The ashes. And: the cut.

THE COLLEGE

for Janet Rodney, y los demas . . .

. . . Now may all ships be hailed,
now may the call go out—voice on the waters,
now may the men sit down, and women be at peace,
now may all journeys planned be cancelled,
the names of ships erased from lists,
now may insurance be refunded, and gambling cease,
the book of laws and regulations laid aside,
now may the sails be furled, now may the birds
sleep easy on the mast-tips in dawn breeze,
now may the fish follow their schools in undivided waters,
and may all now desist
   from putting lives at peril on the living wave:
for the sun has shone out of the storm
and the berry bushes are white with doves—
          we have found paradise . . .

        coming, under your instructions, my sweet Lord,
upon an island which the inhabitants do call
         "the land far out at sea",
but so pleasing it is to us,
that verily we have left off looking for Eden—
     and, according to your best instructions,
(as aforesaid)
     have seized the land for your wisest uses,
including, to the benefit of the whole people,
 fair *Education,*
       sister to God . . .

Main Street, Nantucket:
     rising out of the sea,
dragon-tooth cobbles
     oiled with thick sperm—

huge shapes at dusk astride the wind,
    (maw-gape, fan of balleen),
  nightmares trawl up
   the venerable shit of whales,
   the incised ivory,
   the jewelry of China
     and paradiso's light—

Friends' Meeting House ╱ Fair Street: Mo. 9 Day 8.   11.40 hours
Brought the sea salt
up in our blood to the land,
              that ancient memory
as of tears, as of salving licks,
  our bellies troubled
under the palms of Africa,
  as of lamentations further back:
winged beings cataracting from the sky,
           thinking already
on the cold space below—
  brought the sea in our blood
as this town has brought its stones
  out of the belly of leviathan,
ballast from England on the mellow streets,
  and the sea runs on the cobbles
(with dancing lights
  your childhood tried to measure)
and back into its bed at night,
  sluicing the dead back from the streets at dawn
the town rocked in her dreams
           below the far Pacific . . .

Evacuate.
Judge the race failed. And take the people out,
eradicate at source the firstborn of America:
     and, according to your wisest instructions,
put faculty in bricks,
servants in clapboards,
students in sloops at sea ╱
          University of Nantucket

to resurrect the State.
And have ideas for business / businesses,
plenty and moneymaking,
shall feed us all.
In "The Brotherhood of Thieves"
downstreet from "The Jarred Coffin",
black velvet and chowder, (best fries on earth)
           planning all this.

Last of the Rodneys: Mo. 9   Day 8,   circa 13.00 hours.
   :this beach, like a mother to me,
like a great breast.
   My sister used to take me prisoner,
and bury me in sand.
I wd. shriek to be let free.
          The land like flesh.
          The measurements:
          grass in the yard, taller than I at first,
          then reaching to my knees,
          then to my ankles,
heights of the sea /
          stature of waves (idem).
The color of the waves, varying so,
a torch on them at night, their changing lights,
          homeland, great mother:
corn of the ocean.

No photograph
can give you, not even architectural
devices can deliver to you—wideangled lenses?—no,
that gold of cobbles—
   and the arms,
the green arms as if sea-delivered,
   but vegetation
as of, perhaps, that Daphne of the Laurels
   (but this is elm),
nothing can give you / of gold, of gloaming,
not even childhood myths of inner light
sprung from the self-born garden at the cunt

of mother Ceres
—her flowered nipples O Initiates!—
nothing can give you . . . any conception . . .

    : perfection of those narrow streets,
of box-like houses,
    their bowel contents
of pearl and diamond,
    perfection of the hedges and the topiary,
perfection of the roses in the gardens
    and but few other flowers at peak of August
                    (O pure, industrious bees!)
last: mainstreet of the cobbles:
    a sunken reef like a long cloud,
    gold pillar lying underneath the sea,
span of the sun drowned in the waves at night,
                O COLLEGIATES!

Maintained in splendor,
pristine, (fierce eye of whale
as tail collapses and head veers to the right
in that one photograph)—
    you would have to go
to deepest wilderness
within the continent
to find such a virginity:
maintained in splendor
by sudden poverty
            (blighted of God
                for the bloodied waters)
then rediscovered
            by the great moneys
—without a single billboard—
            that barricade America
with boards everywhere else:
no other acres in the whole Republic
(*cultured* that is, with buildings on them),
more CITY e'en than Gloucester, pace Charles Olson,
            to show they know

o in their heart of hearts the good life's meaning
                              quote and unquote
tho' wrecking all life else.

Evacuate the people, according to your wisest instructions,
take out the whole polluted race,
march them right back to Kansas, to Oklahoma,
like their victims before them,
burn Minnesota round them, crack California,
bring derricks down: leave them the strip mines and erosions,
let them rot back to coal and fossils—
and take in now the students of the North Atlantic,
    bring in the poor, the hungry, yearning to be free,
    now may all shipping be recalled, the island isolate,
and everything up to the Rockies sink back into the sea.

    Whales undersea—
                    that hell's *nirvana*:
death spouts from the far corners,
mailing up meat and muscle,
ivory teeth, shrimp-armor, bones of birds,
clouds of delicate blood and clots of sludge,
the aromatic dung,
  and all that tint of cobbles
becoming pavings, becoming stones and shingles,
    / the songs dying /
melodious arias, lately recorded,
heard, long and ghost-like, in a night of silver
by ancient fleets:
    / the songs dying /
music unheard
    that would have rocked Nantucket,
made no fortunes at all,
and raised no pillars—
    but a concert of humans and beasts
                              to gladden the world,
    to begin an era,
                    peaceable kingdom
America should be, should have become . . .

136

Mo. 9 Day 9. 21.40 hours.
I work you in the night
        praising the Newfoundland
and Nova Scotia coasts, and coasts of Labrador
        Dorn's Iklavik high on the pole
and Grand Manan.
                    The herring fleets.
A million fish in the smoking-houses.
The sun swinging the pivot of Machias Seal
        as far as green Monhegan.
Great eagles battering the doors of the new world
                    at Cape Breton.
Where Cabot, and so forth.

        Wherefore we mourn
New Brunswick towns ripped out by open highways,
Maine littered with motels,
Cape Cod lost in a maze of villas,
        the Vineyard sullied,
the obsolescent ferry-boat betrayed to knackers
they'll want for a museum shortly afterwards,
all our pathetic, short-lived history,
two hundred years for sale, or trash, or garbage,
        so soon, would you believe it?

Dawn up, thru Main Street one last time,
towards perfection pristine in the whaler's eye,
down to the steamer wharf.
        The dying ferry's still. Far out to sea,
a sky born out of blood, just pink as yet.
        Now we are older than the old world is,
our people wiser.
                And where we had imagined,
from all engravings seen, a whole Atlantic,
and a Pacific, giving up their ships,
bringing to harbor
        an elegance of masts, a soaring choir
of sails all home in peace:
        one daughter on the surf, round,

pregnant-white,
    twin-towered *Shenandoah,* corn-girl of ocean,
wise as adventure, rocks on the risen pearl.

Now as the spider toileth on the sun
gliding around its web, our ponderous ferry boat,
a recent model whose name I've lost,
slides round the sleek one
Mo. 9 Day 10. 07.30 hours,
                as she in sleep,
    running for Mystic now with all our dreams
              makes fast to memorize

the anchorage of Eden . . .

THREE NARRATIVES

NARRATIVE OF THE SPIDERS

for Asa Benveniste

I

The spider, as I dial a number,
hanging in the air beside me, moving with slow
exploring at the air her long forelegs, climbing the air,
the invisible hair she has spun out
of her own body, swimming an invisible sea,
where is she going, seemingly *up* to me,
and yet perhaps for her some other travel—
the spider sailing her own world,
along her own tracks
in latitudes she alone understands.

The irony—that I should have become
father to a house of spiders
as if I'd had innumerable daughters
spun from my mind alone.
No cranny in the house but has
its spider: they even nest behind the pictures
and inside books. In my own paths
I come upon them suddenly: not all the education
I've tried to give myself in their regard
prevents that shudder at their sight, and yet,
how calm they are at their navigation
and sleeping in their havens!

And it is not as if they were the large
tropical horrors I've known elsewhere, squatting like
disembodied hands on beds, or curling legs around
a windowsill: the stage-shy ballerinas. They are small
for the most part, and probably do little harm
to others of their kind within the house. Tho
I have caught, in a glass, one black, to put it out,
and then a white, and suddenly there was, there were not two,
but one black spider crouching in the glass. We must know
our thoughts, which goes with which,
and which will eat the other like a witch.

Fall. Great lines in the sky, thick and black,
as if drawn with the brush of a Japanese master,
constantly re-arranging themselves over the fields,
making for South, yet with many a curve,
as if in sleep, or in desire for sleep, to wheel and land,
the whole long V of them, on some round pond,
or down the length of the sea-longing river.
Their ways are also set apart. Their noise is the most
mysterious the night knows, they conjure travel,
essence of movement. Above the house, out in the fields,
and further out into the hungry world,
some part of mind will always go with them, will be forever
travelled in their flight. As if a web of flyways in the night
covered the earth with programs. Process of their flight,
and process of the poem now made one, an ancient ritual
haunting like movement to me, come to rest.

Now the geese gone. Whereas, within the house,
within the mind, as I would criticize
the notebooks I've not written, and the poems
time has not had me for—these galley slaves, the spiders,
weaving who knows what silks and what brocades
I might in other voices weave, if I could find
the whole plan of their movement, in and out of season,
and when they will appear on a calm night, and not appear
on nights of rain when most to be expected. Syntax of fright,
clearing the way for knowledge. Which can't be fear,

140

is that not so, and which can only be the beauty of my daughters
as they are born, mine as they trick to dress,
mine as they die, their frail legs closed at last
around the bitter heart that could but father them,
and then leave them to fate, the cold night, or the broom.

II

The sunglasses I had lost all weekend
found at last at the bottom of my satchel
on which everything I had in the world was piled,
broken at the bridge. Glasses cannot break worse.
The voice of Alegria saying
''You no longer need dark to look at light''.

And there is too much in the world
that cannot be married, or conjunct, or cemented in union
of any kind. How shall I then take the pure light
from my faithful, lifelong friend beside the bed
telling me to recognize myself in it and not fear,
and how not fall headlong, past all the brides,
lovers, fellows, acquaintances, down to the last
slip of the lizard's feet on the greasy tree,
over the skull and thru the eyes
into the world of spiders?

Expecting the great spider at the mind's edge
to come like a telephone-call in the silent house,
suddenly, among the empty walls, along the bare rafters
and be so large she will engulf the house
like a call engulfs silence, changing biography,
bringing the future into life. Alegria said
''Mother''. I said: ''No, daughters''. The spider
which will be death—and will be, also, love.

My body cannot digest my soul tonight and I am left
a house of winds. ''It is not necessary'' Alegria said
''to cut the string of the kite when it explores the sky,

but merely to get used to the lengthening of the string
and all the places it goes.'' And the string
trembles to a thousand voices like a harp
with but one string. The harp with a thousand strings
is of no use to me; it is broken at the bridge like
my glasses. The kite has gone to meet its fellows in the sky.
Winds sing in the wires of the old plane,
two officers in formal dress are not height sick, one
bellows into the ear of the other thru a megaphone,
the pilot calmly taking his suggestions. ''Cut off the engines''
Alegria said ''and took me thru my fears one by one,
cut off the engines, dived perpendicularly, surfed on clouds,
made me feel my body weightless, brought in the radio
to elucidate the voices of the clouds''.

''And below the sea, there was a blue crab,
weaving a blue, plastic-like substance out of its tail
which then became a shell or imperial palace
the mad blue weaver lived in. Took my camera out
to find the crab I'd seen, but could not do so
and the old fisherman I'd left behind, who'd lived
many a higher life in vain and now had chosen this
to watch for men, he laughed: the grin took out his face
he laughed so much when I returned to port.''

III

Uneasy, in the slip of making, yet thought for once
moving to its appointed end like a hunter.
The voices outside have sounded for three days
and have been woven into one skein. The skein is inwards
now, sinking into the sea like a crab, and the sound
falls into deeper and deeper blues under the waves.
Blue line on a deep blue bed. The line follows,
among the ten thousand things of the sea, picking out
unerringly and, tho I do not know it with the reel,
those things which match the discourse. Alegria sings
with bright eyes in the mind, it is the eyes that sing.

142

I have feared movement all my life, feared walking, feared
dancing also, feared height and depth, the air, the sea
and the path before me. Did I fall once, this fall, or in
some other fall? As I saw my daughter once,
sprawled on the floor when she was very little
—and the sudden howl as she dropped from bed unseen
to be found on the floor? I fear the spiders
because they are there without having appeared to come
where they now are, which is: not up in the sky, but here,
in the house with us. They are my movements, those
I've not moved, but moved nevertheless, thru passage
of this time I am allotted. I fear my daughters,
my actions, the blind women moving thru the poem
that cannot come to birth until their mother is exhausted.
They are spiders, in delicate blue dresses, they are crabs,
they are not yet the birds in the air in the indigo night.

Do the birds achieve? Watch the birds move, on the wing,
perching, or feeding now among the molluscs of the pond.
Can you imagine a bird, relaxing in the grass, one knee
over the other, smoking a cigarette, let's say inactive?
This passion for achievement, to tear it from a life, impossible.
Though nausea attend it—impossible still.
Once, I found a web at the door, moving slightly in the morning
wind and destroyed it. By the evening, the web had been
woven again exactly as before. I was so moved, I left it.
Destroyed. Nature is careless. Build now. It is but life.

NARRATIVE OF THIS FALL

for Robert Duncan

I do not ask for the rain to come down.
Silence. We begin with the silence and then, softly,
the rain comes down, not to argue, not to educate,
but to fall.

The light has been left on upstairs.
Downstairs. This is where
the writing materials are, where I write,
and the light upstairs is as much there
for returning unto
as it is there to enable it to fall, downstairs.

The light is below us, underfoot. It has come down
in the shape of leaves from the Norway Maple,
to argue the price of gold. Gold has not any price
when set beside these leaves. This gold will be
a short time, before it turns to dust,
first solid dust, then less and less solid,
though sand lasts a long time. That lasting is not
what we are asking here, but the price of a moment,
the price of pure yellow, unalloyed. The leaves
are not lying flat—taken leaf by leaf—
and there are several thousand leaves,
but, together, they are lying flat as a carpet.
One could think of hands, cupped over each other,
or extended, with fingertips touching. They are a bother
only to birds, who wear hats of leaves
as they scrabble for seed. The light
is below us underfoot as we dance.
Looking up at the trees, I can see their fingers
whose hands I could not see
among the leaves when they were on high.

I am a king of ignorance
trying to look down from the stairs of light
at the floor below. If there is a center
to that floor, none of the dancers upon it
know where the center is.

Some men spend their lives speaking
as if they knew the center of the floor
and the exact location in the ceilings
whence the light floods down
upon each particular square inch of floorboard.
I can get no information from the walls,
indeed I wonder whether there is a room around this floor
which might have walls. Nor are the dancers
in the open air as they are when among leaves.
Dancing. That was the name they had for it
in the old days, tho now it would be called
circumambulation. Which supposes a center.
Which cannot be found.

I am asking certain voices
which seem to fall from on high
and which are not mine that I can recognize,
lodged into my ears from the side as it were,
altho there are no walls, asking the voices whether
they know of any center to this floor.
And they answer me in certain tongues
which, altho I know a good many tongues,
and those among the most ancient of tongues,
I know not the provenience of these.
Dictation. Even the machine I type on
is singing tonight, with a siren hum
trying to drown out the voices. It is clear
that I will have to inhabit this might-be room
a long time
before the center, if there is one, is revealed.

We have a compost of exasperated dissent
in the place where the fresh leaves should be

and which will see no leaves
until next Spring. Break the rhythm
is the next instruction. Manipulate
the under-hand or, more correctly, the underfoot.
I stretch up to no purpose. They shall say to me,
I know, that my voice is a singing one
and that I run the cicada's blood.
If this were the place for sources,
I would argue that no specific blood runs in these veins.
I will have no Chinas here, nor Tibets,
nor Guatemalas, nor Egypts. And I give up
the beautiful scarves falling into the sea
as slowly as the years of my life falling down
this trench of what I am to be.
Even in speaking of them,
singing of them as I do here, I give them up.
They have not, before this, provided the clue
to the presence of the center, thus I deem them
useless. The only odyssey I know
is the rain from the high sky to the low,
via a multitude of intermediate skies,
losing color as it comes down, turning
transparent, losing its voices even,
becoming very silent as it touches earth,
briefly as in an acquaintance's kiss.
On the leaves it makes a little more noise,
but only a little. I know of men
who are in love with machines:
talking machines and singing machines and even
silent machines. They are the kings
of the moment, and besides my ignorance,
their ignorance is like a golden knowledge.

And others erect a Babylon of rain, driving it
up into the skies again thru all the layers,
and the rain takes on their color and their voices,
until we have a Babel out of the Babylon,
besides which no harps can be hung,
since there are no willows. But I will have

no Judaea here either. I will silence the sources.
Sources. Silence. The light still on upstairs.
I could go back upstairs, the night is still young,
listen to the voices I know, some new ones,
and seek comfort from that. I could go
to California, or Alaska, I could travel. I could try
telling you of glaciers and mountains,
lake-formation, the marching to and fro of ice sheets.
Or of whales at sea, humps rising
like islands each time they breathe,
sharks waiting for their blood to fall
when they are wounded. Or of populations
starving the length of the Sahel
which is the length of the arms of the world's body.
We have not enough tears to shed for the Sahel,
we have not even one tear to shed for the Sahel.
I doubt we have a tear for ourselves. The syntactic Sahel.
They ask me often why I love the desert
and I say that the sand is under the sea I love
and I must love the sand.

If this could be . . . an inhabitation. If this could be
like the dead coming to life again and having
affairs with me between the sheets, I would say yes.
If my friends could come down from their portraits
arranged against this wall, and inform me of their actions,
of the joy in their writing, the midnight hours
burning in splendor round their heads, and they were saying
things that would lead me towards the center of this fall,
I would say yes. If their souls
could come out of their bodies, out of their mouths
and ears let us suppose, or out of their navels,
or even out of their cocks and cunts, and say
what makes their pupils round, their irises
color of gold a certain moment in the dusk, then yes.
It is not as if we had no time
for miracles. This boat I lie in
like the sun on the sea going down into death,
this boat floating on the floor of the ocean

a thousand fathoms below this floor, and the whole world
away from my two ears, the whole extent of it
still declares little.

There is a hole in my tongue. In its center.
There are many holes in my mind, my mind is like a sieve.
The soup which is to keep me alive today
falls thru my tongue: I have no nourishment.
I bring my right hand up to my mouth
and speak as if in asides to the other side.
The side from which the voices come, but it can be
the two sides. Confusion. We shall have confusion here
whether we wish it or not. The smoke
rises into my eyes, it is the only thing to rise
in the whole poem. I shall go to my dear one upstairs
and tell her I carry her happiness in my voice
as I would carry corn to broadcast. To scatter seed
in this fall of the year is foolish. Yet we scatter.

I have borrowed this lover from my friends
and will return her when they require it.
One of my friends, no matter which one,
has driven a stone into my central eye. I am lord
of the empire of downstairs unquestionably. With the pain
I see the magnificent crotch of my lover rise
into the light, fire burning there among my fountains.
With the odor of pine and scorched manure she burns,
with alcohol, with opium and broiled meat
above the hills, with shoals of fish below the hills at sea,
alive among the fossils in old sands. She is clothed in leaves.
She never frets. She dances.

The snow will come soon. Winter. Or perhaps
there will be a carpet of sunlight on the naked ground.
There may be mist over the river where I live,
a fishing boat in which I lie and dream.
Sufficient be it to take the gold into the house now,
to express it in the form of a green plant.
The green plant on my desk before me is a Swedish ivy:

148

it grows like riot. I will give you tea
at this table, or coffee, or wine. I will cook for you
at this table and entertain you with mirth
and conversation. You will tell me of times
gone and to come. You will have no voice
but it be peripheral, certainly you will not bring me news
of the hidden kingdom in the center of the floor.
There's a great deal of love in our relationship.
I will weigh your scholars in the palm of my hand,
saying they correspond to this or that knowledge
I have accumulated over the years, and I will tell you
whether their books are true or false. But of the floor,
I will not say a word and you will be unable to likewise.

NARRATIVE OF THE READINGS IN CHICAGO

for David Lenfest

I am smoking three cigarette butts at a typewriter
whose keys are larger than my machine's. I had forgotten
to buy a pack for myself. This butt will not last long
but I should not be smoking.
Goodbye New York, New York. Hello Chicago!

I told the woman I left this morning on the East Coast
about this appartment by the seaside in Chicago.
I love the view from my friend's sitting-room
out onto the beach with the sea in close, and the wild duck
from Canada on the waves. And the planes
like locusts out of Ontario. (From that height
the skyline of the city—wide, menacing,
the forehead of a monster bull with a thousand horns,
seems like a fist, a small fist, held close
to the massive body.) And I also love
the walk along the shore, the city sitting
with its feet in the sea, its heels soaking.
It is November evening now.
Impossible to tell sand from snow, snow from sand.
We know the paths here, we remember them from Summer.
And from the Winter behind that Summer, and from my youth
in this town when neither of us knew the other.

We have brought for each other's examination
the details of this impossible life, a life of scrambling
from chore to chore, overwork, not enough rest, not enough
meditation, too many bodily pains, not enough happiness.
We recite the frustration ritual: now my chapter, now his,
until we have exhausted each other's patience. I have come
to Chicago to give readings, but the intervals between
are crammed with all the things I cannot do in my village:

concerts, art galleries, museums, movies. The skyline
snags at every corner. I like this architectural museum,
I have a soft spot in my heart for it: it has always been so
ever since I was doing my doctorate here at the U. of C.

The people are walking as in a dream towards the beach
between the sand and snow. It is the pollen, bringing its fevers
to mark the turn of the year. They have come foremost
for the ship, tall as the city, that catches them in sleep
and passes them by with frightening showers of joy. The lights
on the ship are like the eyes of angels whose wings
like towers are covered with eyes also, and who shout
"America! America!" and "God Bless Italia!" to the needy.
The women in the rowing boats, waiting for the ship,
have declared their love for all of human kind
and have asked how, time passing as it is, they will find
someone to give that love to in its material form
before their fragile physical beauties have faded.
I am reminded of someone whose beauty is passing,
or so she thinks,
and who asks me daily, in each one of my dreams,
how it is that she is to live with this dying beauty.
I do not know the answer, but I know that I die with her
and that it is going to take me the rest of my life
to become safe.

The boys who dream of these women before their time
trying to lift them into the realm of spirit,
dance in the mist on the pier, each one looking for beauty,
saying softly, under their voices, ashamed each for each,
"Dearly beloved love, how and when shall I find you?"
and the music haunts the boys and those who watch them.
While a man looks up, in the full measure of his powers,
at the great sky of stars, that architecture, and asks
"How is it that this great house of stars remains standing
so long, and who or what is it that keeps it standing?"
As for the girls, they will find lovers one by one
among officials in the surrounding towns, but the boys
will remain bachelors, crying all their lives for their mothers,

and that man will become widowed before he can return
from the picnic to the magic boat where he sighs in the masts
and his brother shouts for his woman among the Summer leaves.

For my part, I will go on to Utah and then to California
for the purpose of giving other readings to pay off lawyers.
I will take the precaution of buying packs of cigarettes
when likely to spend an evening near a friend's machine.
Who knows when lightning will strike, and the poem be born?
When the towering ship will pass in the night
as a white ''Italia'' ship passed me once between Suez and Burma?
Or when I shall be able to lift the sacred woman in my breast
so that she stands at tree-top with my soul, my brother?
Who knows when there will suddenly be no cause for complaint
among the details of this impossible life, and when Chicago
will be playing all its trumpets and all its birds
in a huge service jazz band for the many-fingered city
before I leave fair Illinois and make for Iowa?

And how long my friend will have his appartment
and how long the snow will merge with the sand
before he goes out West, or comes East, or otherwise abandons
the middle earth he has had nine years in his keeping?
Nine years is almost ten. Ten's a decade. When ten comes
the lights in men's eyes may go out, the world cease to breathe,
a blinding smoke issue from railroad stations and airports
and no further occasion for narrative present itself,
the words cold on the ground, beaks gasping, dead of pollution.

VERSE LETTER TO A NOBLE PERSON,
UPON RECEIVING FROM HIM A COMPLIMENT

for Guy Davenport

. . .
Akragas, at the height of our love.
    As I was spinning round with the universe
in the largest available Fiat (black)
          she'd gifted me
that raven Demeter-Persephone
      (mother & daughter in one soul
        and body black,
and hair so black—but that is now so old so let it pass)
    there came
       (her brother-son, and husband thus besides
dying in London of a cancered lung)
    like a black hand
rain down on Agrigento, out of the ruins, rain,
      and out of clouds,
rain still more rain and with a stillness
    as of her eyes in pain
—some way from Noto wrapped in violins, still further from
Segesta's coat of pearl at noon,
too far from Tyndaris where she and I had chased
each other's bodies with our golden souls—
    out of the ruins there opened
out of the bones of earth, I say, that purple flower,
orchis of underworld, purple as vulva
            in the great heat of love

that takes man in under the corn
the maze of death outdone, the labyrinth
outsmarted once for all by the fine thread
         of our ambitious life:

and I PAINTED it,
sitting under an old umbrella, as might some Anglican
lover of nature a century gone by
        depicted it with all the tools I had:
one black felt pen, one violet,
        for dearest life,
                        but for what else
my Dear Guy Davenport
                        wd. one delineate
the Girl's own gift?

II

Reminding me
of marigolds in corn around Pantalica
—the Fiat parked outside the ruins, my station locked
into the arms of time, myself refusing
to give to time that weight and credence
                        foul air demands
but making it
        space, space, as you have said somewhere,
a space of simultaneous joy, in which each had his breath
                        each flower, each man,
& all the paradigms of flowers, & all of men.
                        I wd. have given much
at that dear time, just to behold her eyes
and then crab sandwich and the beer I have
                        writing this letter.
    Had not that chance.
Murdered my wife and children slowly, with the very hands
                caressed her cheeks,
so that, right here,
        there are no children in this kingdom.
                The flower, orchis,
why, but why else, Dear Davenport,
                would one then send
to *Persephone's author,* or to the father of
                Flowers and Leaves,
or to that friend of flight whose dream machines,

the Antoinettes and the Deperdussins,
drone on with ours in paradisal skies
under the hopeful gaze of Kafka's daughter,
such modest texts as stand so much in need
of fathers' benedictions?
                              I have at all times
remembered the fathers painfully, what they have done for us,
the terrible lives led for us, the blood they shed,
under Avernus, and their great deeds we sons alone can sing,
            (& for this labor, do we not,
      for this Ideal Republic?)
and do you say, now,
                              (I am among them) even modestly?
To that: Amen.

III

For the places, and what you say about them:

                              I came upon Kentucky once,
at dawn, far back in nineteen fifty-two, Havana-bound,
it was the morning place. I remember horses
gleaming in fields, under blue hills. The hills were verily
blue. It is the only time I have seen Kentucky. Once
I came out of the Arkansas lakes, bound for Kentucky
but a mist
over Tennessee made me lose my way, and by the time
I had recovered it, Virginia had me.
                        The Girl you see, again.

      As for New Hope, it is Quaker I believe,
and a great place for passage:
Wells Ferry (1722-1747), Canbys Ferry (1748-1764)
Coryells Ferry (1765-1790), New Hope (1791-1974).
In 1810, Benjamin Parry invented a grain-drying process
facilitating the Girl's export to tropical countries.
A good start for an immigrant, is it not, and the street
                        thrown in for saintly measure?
The truth is: it is not very far from Scudder's Falls

155

where E.P. met Mary Moore of Trenton, and an offer
he made of it. We are close to the fathers.
                            And very close
to this foul century: for the place is a tourist trap,
full of idiotic shops, selling trash, with few exceptions,
selling pollution,
and the people pass like vermin thru a schooner's hulk.
There are said to have been artists once :
                            a Samuel Moon
copied David's "Napoleon Crossing the Alps".
We are not very far from the great city, nor far
from the planes at Newark, Philadelphia, J.F.K.,
which will take us out to the furthest borders. I live now
here alone, called on from time to time by a steady, fine,
lovely and loving woman poet whose hair is red.

                            IV

Today: I celebrated the advent of your letter
by going out and spending too much money
                    on aeronautica: to wit
eight Wills' cigarette cards of early birds,
an antique flight-game, 2 inch by 4, a Lindy item,
plus two fantastic postcards of the same ship
"largest, most costly steamer on inland waters of the world"
                    THE SEEANDBEE
that used to ply twixt Buffalo and Cleveland.
Before that, I had been working on Janus
out of Dumézil and Edgar Wind
and, looking again at *Persephone's Ezra,* I see at 162,
Dumézil here, and further on, god Proca
the king of Alba Longa whom Janus bore upon the nymph
who used to run from suitors emprisoned in her cave.
        Such are our synchronicities on this fine day.
But I must tell you that I have no Greek, none whatsoever,
no Latin either: I am a very monster of the ignorance.
Hence my delight that you should find some merit
                    in those poor songs I sent you.

156

V

The work on Janus
is for a prose book I'm writing and calling at this point
Atlantis: An Auto-Anthropology, Part One: The Abundance of Waters.
Abundance of Waters: Atitlan, the name of the holy lake
in Guatemala. Notice the echo: Atitlan / Atlantis.
I am a priest of that lake, not of Eleusis,
    besides, you honor me too much in saying that.
The book is a study in the structure of "Nathaniel Tarn",
only the autobiographical items pertaining to that structure
therein allowed. No blurring of the edges. More towards that, anon.
                    For: *The Artemision,*
it is a fifth part of a new book, due out in March from New Directions
which explores a considerable number of metamorphoses
in a considerable number of cultures, of the Bride of God.
The book is called *Lyrics for the Bride of God.* I got the name
"Artemision" from a dictionary, wanting a term for "Temple of Artemis."
Once saw, in Charlottesville, that a Georgian poet had writ an *Artemision.*
    I am nearly ashamed of such admissions
to a man of your calibre.

VI

There is nothing else to wonder about now,
                my dear Persephonist,
but at this fair conjuncture.
                The fabric of the world
is cracking all about us, her robe is rent
in which she used to rise, Our Girl, from Hades.
They are talking to the plants now, I'm sure you know that?
Tell me: will they save us?
    Look at yr. feet where they stand.
                Will the fathers,
under the ground, and he so lately joined them,
will they be able to save us, as they push,
          the plants up from the ground? Novelty,
novelty, *fads upon Eleusis.*

I have been reading lately Samuel Taylor Coleridge
and wondering yet again, at the beauty,
which comes upon me almost like a storm of tears,
tempest of aspirations in the stillborn mind,
when I read of the travails of those who have gone before us
on the perilous path. Have you felt that?
Light on the leaves: the birds, the systems:
sweet transformations. City of Light, out of Dis arising,
word on the stone, and the stone blessed, and the Girl
running swift-footed on the green lawn, out of sight,
into the arms of her mother. Nothing, in American, yet
quite like it: please say American. That image:
city become a throne /
                              the sanctuary around her hair
whose tresses are alive with light, for me that Paris,
phaetons, white crinolines, clear gaze of waltzes,
born 1928, in rue François Premier
                              that city and that throne
enough to carry us?

                              One more time, as if,
if in her arms, if at the orchis
                              between her royal thighs?

Tonight, I sleep upstairs.

VII

And shall not every night soil, they say,
                              have a morning flower?
Normally, I sleep downstairs. Last night, a spider,
the animal of Hades, larger than most, appeareth in the bedroom:
I try to trap her is my wont, she will not come to trap,
I kill her with a mist. Hatred of this as deep as any hatred,
                              the misery of killing
(imagination of oneself limping under the mist,
the sudden goddess-kick, Fortuna gone right mad,
black whore of Janus spinning above in mist, and I, dying,
          dying at last, incomprehensibly.)
This must be lifted: I sleep upstairs.

158

To make an end of it, for this might never end.
My father is lord of ships and celestial navigations.
Is he not, looking before and aft, sailing right now that sweet river
right up to Jupiter? Beyond all human oceans to that sea of stars
is he not sailing? Wherein our kind shall live in days to come?

                I give you that face of perfection
which looketh into the abyss and seeth the invisible as one,
looketh to the corners of the harried earth,
seeth the visible as many,
                looketh into its own profiles
seeth the many and the one as a single race.
                Passage, passage—all is passage!
We go from earth on fire to a celestial realm of bannerets,
                sole survivors of disaster.
Our ship will bear our brains up to the heavens
that they might fertilize the moon, the Mars canals
                the heavenly wedding bands
of Jupiter. What matter, honest souls, if ships be tribulations?
                if we suffer too much for vision?
if life becomes a hell for us because we see too much?
            In passage, the secret,
in perpetual movement, the secret, in not resting anywhere
                the secret,
in bearing the aspirations to heaven, the secret,
                in seeing one's face in the mirror,
the secret.

An Airport in my dreams: a rush of noise along two channels:
before emplaning, I must see X or Y. Impossible decision.
The two channels scream on shuddering legs.
                Wake calling her, calling her:

the one dragged underground.

. . .

                New Hope, Pa. 12.19.75

Photo: Janet Rodney

Nathaniel Tarn was born in Paris and educated in France, Belgium, and England. He studied History and English at Kings College, Cambridge and subsequently became a journalist in Paris. He then studied anthropology at the Sorbonne and took a doctorate in that subject at the University of Chicago, with field work in Central America. After further study in London, he went to South East Asia at the end of the fifties and subsequently taught at the University of London. He was awarded the First Guinness Prize for Poetry in 1963, then the top award in Britain. In 1967, he left anthropology to create and direct the Cape Editions series at Jonathan Cape and also to found Cape Goliard. In 1969, he taught English at Buffalo and immigrated to the States in 1970, when he taught Romance Languages at Princeton and subsequently Comparative Literature at Rutgers. He lives on the Delaware in Pennsylvania.

The House of Leaves contains all the poems written during the years 1969-1975 except for the work that went into *Lyrics for the Bride of God*, published in 1975 by New Directions. Tarn is now working on a book about Alaska and also on a prose work, the *Atlantis: an Auto-Anthropology. Boundary 2, a Journal of Postmodernist Studies,* recently published a 100 page symposium on his work.

Nathaniel Tarn

Printed July 1976 in Santa Barbara & Ann Arbor
for the Black Sparrow Press by Mackintosh & Young and
Edwards Brothers, Inc. Design by Barbara Martin. This
edition is published in paper wrappers; there are 200 copies
numbered & signed by the author; & 26 lettered copies
handbound in boards by Earle Gray each containing an
original drawing by Nathaniel Tarn. *55*